CROFTER

A Wyoming Homestead Manual
and Radical Memoir,
Rooted in Place

Renée Carrier

BRAEBURN CROFT AND PRESS

HULETT, WYOMING

Cover Painting, "Light on the Horizon," by Joan Fullerton. www. JoanFullerton.com

Author photo by AdriAnne Graaff

ISBN 978-1-7340437-3-0

In support of the ethics of bioregionalism, sustainable food production, herbalism and civil, civic responsibility, with abiding respect for all those who came before and to come, this publication is intended to provide educational information for the reader on the covered subject. It is not intended to take the place of personalized medical counseling, diagnosis and treatment from a trained health professional.

Library of Congress Number: 2022923593

Published by BRAEBURN CROFT *and* PRESS
824 HIGHWAY 112, HULETT, WYOMING 82720
(307) 467-5930

Permission granted to author to use "Widening Circles" by Rainer Maria Rilke, translated from the German by Joanna Macy and Anita Barrow

Also by Renée Carrier

Non-fiction

A Singular Notion

Novels in *The Riven Country* Series

The Riven Country of Senga Munro

Starwallow

The Simpler

Compiled further material, edited, and published a manuscript by the late S. Paul Latiolais, Col. USAF Ret., the author's father (1920-2004).

STRAIGHT AND LEVEL, The True Story of a Young Man's Quest to Become a Flying Cadet in the U. S. Air Corps

With love for André, DiDi, Gabi, Felicia, Alex, Nancy, and, for Micheline, in memory.

Widening Circles

I live my life in widening circles
that reach out across the world.
I may not complete this last one,
but I give myself to it.

I circle around God,
around the primordial tower.
I've been circling for thousands of years
and I still don't know:
am I a falcon, a storm, or, a great song?"

~Rainer Maria Rilke

*Translated from the German
by Joanna Macy and Anita Barrow*

v

Figure 1 Plantings and Gardens Map

CROFTER

FOREWORD

We are all of us born, I think, with a longing to be one with the land. Even as we make our livings in the concrete forests of a city, for many of us there comes a time when the call to return to a quieter, more natural way of life becomes so loud it must be heeded.

When Renée approached me to edit this book, her intent was simply to create something helpful to be passed on to the next owner of her land: a thriving orchard with a view that stretches to every horizon, here in the northeast of Wyoming. Part memoir and part manual, it was to be "useful".

But as I began to read through the chapters, I realized it was so much more. Woven through the recipes and detailed instructions for watering apple trees and tending the vegetable garden is Renée herself. Her personal history is so entwined with the land and what caring for it has taught her that the two cannot be separated.

As Renée needs to feel the soil with her fingers, to nurture both soul and mind, so the land needs her tender care to flourish, in partnership with her equally wonderful husband, Jeff. *Crofter* is a tale of timeless symbiosis: the relationship between humans and the earth that gives us life.

I moved to this corner of the world from England's largest metropolis, after years of wistfully reading magazine articles about planting my own potatoes. Alas, it was not to be, for no London home has room for an honest garden.

As I read *Crofter,* all that yearning rushed back to me. I've often been asked what possessed me to move from a capital city with all its modern conveniences to a tiny, rural community where the nearest cinema is a 40-minute drive down the interstate. I may, in future, simply hand my interrogator a copy of *Crofter.*

In an era of global warming, heightened political tensions and war, Renée reminds us that life at its core is simple. What you take, you must replace. What nourishes you must be offered nourishment in return. What you give of yourself will always be returned.

Perhaps not all of us will have the chance to harvest apples and garlic grown with our own hands, but we can all stand to learn a little something about the umbilical cord that links us to the world we call home. And so, I convinced Renée that her manual has value to more than just her heirs.

There are lessons within this book for us all about finding fulfillment, and true peace.

Sarah Pridgeon

PREFACE

Homestead: *1. a dwelling with its land and buildings, occupied by the owner as a home, and exempted by law from seizure or sale for debt; 2. any dwelling with its land and buildings, from the Old English hāmstede—for home and place. According to the 1967 American College Dictionary.*

Croft: a small plot of land, often with a house, especially in Scotland. Encarta Dictionary.

As crofters and keepers of a homestead (by the second definition, rather than governed by the 1862 Homestead Act), my husband and I safeguard an heirloom for a future generation. The role of caretaker charges us to maintain the land and place we call "home." Yes, just so. The gods of posterity, or the like, proposed an operating manual for our place, there being too many areas, procedures, chores, concerns and minutiae to leave to chance, and no guide for whoever settles here after us—perhaps one of the children or grandchildren, perhaps not. They have chosen different livings, though each relish their visits. Think, "Retreat House."

The following occasionally reads as memoir, radically rooted in time *and* place, if you'll forgive the pun, as well as a working chronicle. A natural history of place arises by default. Outnumbered by flora and fauna, rocks and rills, we are protected by a sheltering bone structure of the very land.

My intent is to offer explanations, or suggestions, to ease, tease and entice a satisfactory—nay, *fulfilling*—living; further, a sustainable life. I will attempt to clarify what we have found necessary to do and, finally, to share what we have discovered works and what may not. When I say, "living," I mean a day-to-day way of life—not one solely engaged in *earning* that living off the land. Retirement and social security incomes free us to pursue a rustic contentment, as it were, in an area of the country where, prior to Internet, far less opportunity for non-essential expenses existed—longer drives to larger towns notwithstanding. We derive a small income from selling apples, grapes, garlic and shallots, some years more than others. "*Walking-around* money," my father would have said. "Mad" is another adjective, and one I've heard tossed about ourselves. . . .

Caveat: The effort entailed in maintaining such a place might well serve to question our judgment and sanity, but I don't want to sound smug. Life throws just enough curve balls anywhere you choose to live.[1] I will cover essential homestead maintenance and, sometimes the harder task, propose means to allow for the nurturing aspects of the place.

I organize tasks by season, although it will appear obvious that spring, summer and fall bear the brunt of them. Apart from shoveling snow, winter requires its own, more philosophical set of instructions. Falling in the patent category of hopes and dreams, it is a perfect time to peruse seed catalogues, attend to and practice pastimes, self-reflect or navel-gaze, if that is your wont.

Braeburn Croft
Wyoming, Autumn 2022

---

[1] My husband Jeff has endured four back surgeries; the latest, in October 2018. I underwent open-heart surgery in 2010. I mention these only insofar as they affected our lives to a much greater degree than the usual setbacks. The Covid-19 pandemic presented a further danger.

LOVERS LEAP

The year 2020, a watershed year in worldly affairs, marked our thirty-fourth in this corner of Wyoming. I mark my fiftieth in the state—a "Jubilee Year," of being married to a notion. In explanation, having enrolled at the University of Wyoming in the fall of 1971 to study forestry, I settled on French, but my initial bucolic interest survives.

The northwest limen of the Black Hills is home.

The great, green-black forest naturally ignores state boundary lines with South Dakota. This biome extends farther south, past Newcastle, Wyoming. If I were to guess, I would say the state enjoys only a tenth of what has been called "an island of green" in the plains. Before the Black Hills National Forest resumes its eye-soothing mantle of ponderosas, bur oaks, ash and cottonwoods (among myriad other species), eastern U.S. and western species meet here in a head-long crash of populations. You will benefit from a copy of *Plants of the Black Hills and Bear Lodge Mountains,* by Gary E. Larson and James R. Johnson, regional guides.

The Hills break up just west of Spearfish, leading into Wyoming, to allow for the aptly named *red racetrack,* a geological feature that girds them. The name is taken from "The Great Race," a Lakota origin story. The animals, and those representing humans, held a contest to see who was the most powerful among them. The red color of the track is said to be their blood. The Bison won.

I must here make full disclosure. As inhabitants of the Black Hills, we live on 1851 Treaty Lands recognizing the Lakota and Arapaho as rightful dwellers on the land.

This treaty, and the one signed in 1868, were broken by the American government. To my mind we are doubly charged with caretaking, though our place lies on "unceded adjoining territory." (See *Smithsonian Magazine*, November 7, 2018, article by Kimbra Cutlip.)

Figure 2 Lovers Leap

In 1986, Jeff accepted a position as principal at the local K-12 school. He would later accept the county schools' superintendency for fifteen more years before retiring. An early migrant to the state, he was born in Oklahoma City and moved west with his family when he was only months old. So, pretty much a native. Jeff grew up in Casper and we met at the university in Laramie. His geologist father found in me a willing listener to his explanations of uplifts, calderas and hogbacks.

Eventually, we moved north from Douglas, Wyoming—our home for nine years and where our children were born. Our little house sold quickly but, there being no rentals where we were going, we bought a trailer and had it hauled to a peaceful, cottonwood-shaded mobile home park on the Belle Fourche (*foosh!*) River near town. Our four-year-old son John was in the throes of a chickenpox outbreak. He was a trooper and, behind us, rode up with a friend, who graciously transported some of our things in a borrowed horse trailer. *Thank you, Harv.*

We happened onto the property nine months later by stroke of luck. Situated between two ridges, with the normally dry Little Sourdough Creek splitting the land to the west, we fell in love at first sight as it murmured sweet nothings to us. The holding wasn't on the market per se, but the town's banker had caught wind of it. Later, someone offered the seller a greater sum than he had already agreed from us, and I waged desperate battle with my fountain pen to make our plea in a letter— what we wished to do with his homestead, if permitted to acquire it. He honored our initial agreement. *Thank you, Malcolm.*

We packed up and moved on a chilly, sunny day in mid-March of 1987, driving north from the sweet hamlet of Hulett, away from the Belle Fourche River valley, to an elevation of 4,000 feet, only three miles from where the broken, hilly land touches the lip of the northern plains. Except for the seasonally dry creek beds and cedar breaks, the landscape north mostly flattens out again.

The previous owners had installed electricity, and a well had been dug—two of the larger expenses in developing a property. They lived on the place only a short time, as the gentleman suffered health concerns. That the house was a mobile home did not deter us. Mr. Bucher had built a two-car garage beside it. The two-track, third-of-a-mile road leading from the highway proved in dire need of crowning and gravel, but this was merely another task to jot on the growing to-do list.

Over the years we endeavored (the suitable word) to create a home-grown living, and if this sounds pretentious or too airy-fairy, I beg forgiveness. In my collection of short essays, *A Singular Notion*, published in 2006, I introduced the place I had named Braeburn Croft. I repeat the significance here, as germane: Jeff grew up on Bonnie Brae Street in Casper, Wyoming. My grandparents' last name was Blackburn. Borrowing part of both—brae, for hillside, in Gaelic; and burn, for creek—both figured in our histories. As stated, a croft is a small home with (possibly) a bit of land. We lacked the mule, but gained the acreage, for those who recognize the reference.

As a member of an Air Force family, I had lived a nomadic life, which only paused after my father retired in Georgia. By 1987, I had decamped sixteen times and was keen to settle. I was homesick for it. It is hard, if nigh impossible, to bloom when your roots are yanked from the soil on a regular basis. In respectful defense of my fellow military brats (I *see* you), and those tasked with similar circumstances, some of the prettiest and hardiest flowers grow in the Arctic.

I don't mind that I'm an invasive species. Several of my favorite herbal allies belong to the group, such as dandelion. Apples were also first introduced by settlers. Belonging is a powerful need.

One week after we moved in (*thank you, Karl and Holly, for your help that day*) more than three feet of heavy, wet snow fell, during what we would come to call The March Equinox Storm (or Blizzard), prompting a *what-have-we-done* shiver. Only metaphorically. We cozied up in our rabbit warren, my nickname for the long house, even now. Our home and its environs have since evolved and the initial snowy apprehension was short-lived in favor of the splendid scenery, a long-last promise to ourselves and call to adventure. Our daughter was eight and caught our enthusiasm, for which I am exceedingly grateful. Had she not, it might have proven an unfeasible venture, in terms of abetting her little brother's experience.

In the coming months, we came to realize and accept that we would remodel the existing structure instead of removing it to build a new home—an alternative not in our budget.

Decades ago, during a visit with his sister and her husband, Jeff and I admired a coffee table book in their home. *Handmade Houses* was the title; ours wasn't that, but by the time we added a den to the south, another bedroom and bath to the north and a covered back porch; tied the den roof to the garage by several translucent, fiberglass panels to create a studio/atrium; remodeled the kitchen and first bathroom; and installed two wood stoves, we deemed the *handmade* designation practically appropriate. These improvements occurred slowly over the years, of necessity.

A stable, with chicken coop attached, was raised with the help of friends and family. Corrals, the fencing of pastures and digging a refuse pit occupied our time over several years. The trash pit is thankfully no longer in use. A monthly service now hauls away our refuse, minus sorted recyclables taken to Rapid City.

We have raised sheep, horses, chickens, Guinea fowl and turkeys. We have loved five dogs; Ned, the stubborn but noble Chesapeake Bay retriever; Kate, the sweet Lab mix; Eddy, a Jack Russell Terrier (one of the foxier dogs I've ever known); and the latest, a yellow Lab named after one of my literary characters, Gabe. We once fostered our son's dog, Cessna, for several months.

Cats have come and gone, but my favorite (which translates, *he actually liked me and wanted to cuddle*) was a black, Persian-like breed I named Blackie.

Over the years, we planted vines and shrubs, and nearly a hundred trees (both deciduous and evergreen); however, beside the lane, half-way to the highway, stands a single indigenous bur oak tree. On close inspection, it appears to be several, as multiple trunks grow in a close circle due to the species' root system (and so, maybe not so singular.) Two of the trunks have withered, but from afar the tree resembles a single, great specimen. It garners extra water from the drive's run-off, and reigns as the only deciduous tree in the front field, where volunteer ponderosa-people have sprung up. Beneath the oak rest Sister, a thoroughbred mare; Zaraba, our long-lived Arabian mare; the aforementioned Ned and Cessna. A box holding Eddy's ashes will be buried when we're ready. Never least, the cats, Blackie and Izzy.

A bench invites contemplation. In Beryl Markham's book about her African childhood, *West with the Night,* she writes, "Rest ye well, Buler." Her beloved dog. An intention hounds me—to inscribe a plaque with something similar; to assign reverence and remembrance to the spot, as a place to pause, to take stock, to murmur thanks.

The children have left home. Flown the coop. Jumped over the proverbial moon years ago. Jeff and I continue to live our "home-grown living," with something approaching intention, perhaps merely dogged perseverance—the occasional travel and too-long passages between familial visits notwithstanding. We have three grandchildren, two grand-dogs and two grand-cats. Hearts and loving arms—long and short—stretch across 1,200 miles to the west and 800 miles to the east. We stand as fulcrum. Speaking of kin, may I risk an eccentric suggestion and include the orchard trees, gardens, herbs, flowers and wild things among our family? Which brings me to a further purpose of this manual. . . .

To those of you who find yourselves here one day—either, here, literally, or metaphorically, on another homestead and seeking information—I offer the following with the modest hope that you may find something of use in it.

To everyone else, may you glean some nuggets of interest and inspiration. It has certainly been, and continues to be, interesting and inspiring to live among trees, Rufous-sided Towhees, American Goldfinches, Common poorwills—and more—in the sweeping shadow of Devils Tower ten miles away, and here, below a landmark named Lovers Leap, no apostrophe. I read it as simple observation and a call to action.

SPRING
Wake Up! Or Not

Depending on where you grew up, when you read "Spring," you may conjure daffodils, birdsong and green grass. In northern Crook County, Wyoming, you will, perforce, wait longer. Traditionally, the last official frost date is May 15, and nature has (pretty well) respected this rule. Understand you could get three feet of snow on the fourteenth, in which case you'll be scrambling outdoors to rescue fragile blooms in the orchard and to remove the burden from the branches. It's triage, always, in this circumstance. If you keep animals, they will need to be tended as well.

Early on March 21, as the sun peeks over the eastern ridge (our *yardarm*), stand away from the shadow of the Leap, and brandish skyward a long staff or straight pole. The shadow cast by it will fall due east/west. *Equinox* means equal night (and day), but on this 44th parallel of latitude, the phenomenon is disappointingly skewed. Now, at the equator. . . .

The temperature read twenty-eight degrees at six-thirty a.m. *Warming up to snow,* we both decided, and the following day it did—four inches. Spring means snow here, normally heavier with moisture than in winter, and this requires a fair amount of shoveling of the drive and cement parking pad. A snow shovel and strong back can clear the parking area quickly, *if* the white stuff hasn't been allowed to accumulate; still, we generally wait until the snow has stopped falling. Jeff uses the trusty red tractor to plow the lane. Before we bought The Red Dragon, a neighbor did this for us, the soul of kindness. Our tractor is a smaller beast than Art's and can take up to two hours to complete the cold chore.

Stack firewood beside the garage, never against it, as it invites insects—termites and bark beetles, among others—to set up housekeeping in your home's walls. Wood fuels the efficient stove in the den, the room's only source of heat, and so, we aim to put up about two cords a year, if not more. Noting any telltale dead tree on the property, we'll fell it and use the chain saw to cut it up. An enterprising area resident arrives each year, his mechanical log splitter in tow, to provide an invaluable service. Kenny also brings a load of discarded 4x4 pallet "stays" from the sawmill (lengths used to separate pallet bundles). For now, we don't have to use the axe and hatchet as we did for many years, except for kindling. A second wood stove stands in the master bedroom, for use in emergencies. The power can (*and will*) go out on occasion. Normally, not for long.

I begin with the orchard, mainly because it is an abiding object of our affections and figured in our younger fantasies. The poet Leonard Cohen, our courtship's troubadour, composed the song,

Figure 3 Apple Blossoms Sweeten the Air

"So Long, Maryanne," about growing apples on a farm,

and keeping "all the animals warm." It inspired us, and while Jeff does the lion's share of orchard upkeep and general grounds-keeping (when not laid up by back pain—yes, the corollary is obvious), my farm wife contributions appear in the following two seasons. Of concern, as we age, is the notion of keeping up with the load. Two of us can manage the gardening now, and I content myself with that. On occasion, I hire help with the housekeeping, and we have sought help when needed elsewhere.

As of this writing, in 2022, we count twenty-one apple trees, nine cherry trees, three plums, two pears and thirteen cherry bushes, as well as several wild plums, currants, and gooseberries. Saskatoon berry too—the fruit resembles a blueberry, but with a more intense flavor. Before her fruit sets on, I spray the bush with a solution against powdery mildew. It works beautifully (see REMEDIES.) The orchard demands different chores, depending on the fruit. The row of domestic Nanking cherries and chokecherries along the south fence of the front yard may wait to be pruned of dead limbs after leaves appear. Each year sees some winter kill; that's life.

Apples and Cherries, Plums and Pears; Lions and Tigers and Bears, oh my!

By late April to early May, all fruiting trees must have been pruned for growth. The task may be done any time after leaves have fallen, or before budding. Jeff does it in late March or April with bow saw, pruners, and toilet bowl wax to smear on the larger cuts *(think Band-Aid)*. His calves ache from climbing up and down the ladder. (*Think horse liniment or St. John's Wort and/or arnica oil; these also minimize the hand-strain from gripping pruners.)*

Diagrams for proper pruning technique may be found in several of the references available. Later, after leafing, *any* dead will be apparent. Coco Chanel once famously advised, "Before you leave the house, look in the mirror and take one thing off." In this case, that errant twig, springs defiant, vertically up the middle.

The apple trees are given names (*my fancy, not Jeff's*). In alphabetical order, beginning with the one nearest the stable lane on the western edge of the orchard, they follow a somewhat spiraling pattern in their planting (among the cherries and plums). Meet the goddesses Athena, Baubo, Ceres, Diana, Europa, Flora, Gaia, Hera, Io, Juno, Kalypso, et cetera.

The Exquisite Apple has been maligned, and possibly mistaken, in certain scripture. The Judeo-Christian "forbidden fruit" may actually have been a pomegranate, owing to its association with Hades. Legend has it that those who ate of it when visiting (or being held captive) were cursed to remain part of the year (a stipulation adopted for fairy land visits). But it could well have been an apple. The species originated in the mountains of Kazakhstan thousands of years ago. Eating of the fruit of the Tree of Knowledge of Good and Evil landed Eve, and Adam, "east of Eden." Tricky—when the Earth is round—so, meaning "everywhere." When Earth was believed flat, folks didn't realize you could keep on walking and eventually wind up back in Paradise. On many levels I hope this is still the case, but I digress. . . . (You didn't really believe this manual would be restricted to homestead maintenance?)

After pruning, we find it simpler to rake or pick up the twigs and make piles beside the trees. This procedure may take several weeks. It's a lovely sight, worthy of an impressionist's brush—rustic evidence of industry and care. Jeff uses the chipper to grind twigs and branches into mulch, then spreads it around the base of existing trees to provide nourishment. It has *exactly* what they need, according to Michael Phillips, the author of *The Holistic Orchard.* **Wear gloves and eye protection.** The contraption is hauled around the yard and orchard behind the yard tractor (mower) by its very own adaptor/hitch.

- Just after bud break, and again during blooming (about ten days later), Jeff sprays the trees with *Streptomycin,* against blight. Unfortunately, the organic farming certification gods have chosen to restrict use of the drug. We judge the antibiotic a necessary step, having regretted the sad results of not using it. Trees with blight take on the painful, near-appearance of leprosy; the bark falls off in scaly pieces, and a substance, like phlegm or lymph, oozes from the infected limbs. These must be cut off with a repeatedly disinfected saw (a weak dilution of Clorox). Jeff mixes the inoculants and water in a large tank that sits on the back of the 4-wheeler, then he dons a mask and goes a-sprayin'. Best to do early in the morning before the wind kicks up, on a day when chance of rain is nil.

I invite you to discern fragrance from mere smell. Spring breezes carry scent molecules and the effect in an orchard is (on the whole) perfectly lovely. The fragrance of the plum blossom is a favorite, while pear blossoms smell, to me, like stinky socks. I don't know how they manage to be pollinated. At all. No offense, Dear Pear, and forgive my human-biased observation. Like the ugly duckling tale, the fruit proves the overall grand scheme.

Resources in the home library describe standard orchard practices, theories, et cetera, but I wish to categorize necessary tasks, with these references pointed to, in case. Further orchard chores will be outlined in the summer and fall chapters.

Grapes

- The "Lower Vineyard," as identified, is planted in several varietals, most of which are *Vitis labrusca,* or Fox grape. We believe they have been crossed with Betas, and they do produce a good jelly and juice grape; however, not-so-good a wine. "Foxy" describes the taste (*not* sexy) due in large part to the stronger tannins. Toward the northern end of the rows, we've planted several *Vitis vinifera* varietals, i.e., Maréchal Foch and Sabre-Voix, among others. These are tagged for identification. We harvested enough in 2019 to make wine. It's "working" now, a rhythmic bubble escaping the airlock.

- Labrusca vines create leafy bowers throughout the yard and they garland the front porch. These also benefit from yearly pruning—if you don't want to wind up with an impossible tangle when trying to harvest the grapes in the fall. Count forward from the main stem, to the second or third node of the new branch, and snip it off there. Don't be alarmed when you see a drip-drip-dripping of sap (*think plasma—or don't*) at the cut end of the vine; this is normal and will eventually cease. The leavings may be gathered for grapevine wreaths and/or mulched for their nutrients. My husband derives what some might call "primordial" satisfaction in grape husbandry, however work-intensive it may prove.

The Gardens

At present, several plots are dedicated gardens: a large one near the orchard; the "kitchen garden" behind The Garage (not to be confused with The Shop, which houses more tools, storage space, tractor, old camper, and pick-up); a long, narrow strip called, provocatively, The Witch's Garden—for herbs and flowers. It contains several species grown in every self-respecting green-witch's garden: rue, sage, valerian, motherwort, St. John's Wort, mint, California poppies and, for now, sheep sorrel—all perennials.

Beds in front of the house, and beside the parking area, provide medicinal beauty and more mint, Veronica, Bouncing Bet, edible (yes!) violets, catnip, and roses. In April and May, you will undoubtedly notice the dandelions. Their leaves, most tender in early spring, are good for the liver after a winter's stodgy diet. The roots concocted, meaning simmered long, are a tasty substitute for coffee. Not my cup of tea, however. I ~~like~~ *adore* the taste of real coffee.

Two plots are tilled every year before planting. You may choose to adopt the growing practice of no-till gardening by using a broad fork. It has been suggested, and proven, that fewer weeds seem to take hold, though the soil must still be loosened to avoid compaction. I like to add annuals to each garden for color and insect control (petunias and zinnias for the former, geraniums and marigolds for the latter). A purely personal choice.

The largest plot is divided in two. The garlic and shallot crop, planted in October, matures over winter, and their 1,000-plus heads are harvested in July. But in spring, when the leaves are growing, Jeff uses the small cultivator between the rows at least once. More on garlic in the summer section.

Invaded by a particularly obstinate species of native grass, with thick rhizome-like roots, the struggling strawberry bed was taking much longer to weed—and bear—than it might have. Certain roots manage to choke less-hardy neighbors, resulting in fewer berries. In nature, the stubborn roots have an important purpose— to allay erosion and hold things together—like a determined pioneer mother or a headstrong sailor on a

Figure 4 Jellies and Jam Sweeten Everything

family tree. Thick roots hold more water as well. But in our present berry bed, these were discouraging. Jeff patiently completed the odious weeding task earlier this spring. Fewer ripe strawberries found their way to our kitchen counter.

I freeze them, or make jam, when there are enough, but they are best when eaten fresh and still warmed by the sun. The "daughters," or runners, shooting from the mother plants on umbilical cord-like stems, may be replanted as they appear. Jeff at last decided to remove the strawberries to a new home, below the first, where the soil is more hospitable. After several passes with the rototiller, and much pulling of the unwelcome roots, the bed is improved.

We experiment with different mulches. The name *straw*berry offers a clue, and the instances we lay down pine straw (dry pine needles), the plants flourish. Our soil is terribly alkaline. The pine straw releases acid to correct soil pH. Plain old oat straw, a wonderful mulch, doesn't achieve the same result, though it protects berries from dirt. Six of one, half dozen—

CRUNCHY GRAVEL

I was born a so-called *military brat* on the spring equinox at Boling Air Force Base in Washington D.C. We lived in Alexandria, Virginia, across the Potomac. I'd rather hail from Virginia than the District of Columbia— Owen Wister's novel partly to blame. His Virginian moved to Wyoming, too (with apologies for the false distinction). Dad was a colonel in the Air Force and serving at the time as an advisor to the Joint Chiefs of Staff at the Pentagon. He wrote speeches for Ambassador Henry Cabot Lodge.

In 2001 I received a birthday letter, postmarked Georgia, where he and Mom stayed on after his retirement. In the letter, he reminded me of my birth date's second personal significance. Getting along in years by then, he often commented on various anniversaries beginning to crowd the calendar. His memory was prodigious, as I noted in his aviation memoir, *STRAIGHT AND LEVEL: The True Story of a Young Man's Quest to Become a Flying Cadet in the U.S. Air Corps.* On March 21, 1937, he entered the Corps' flight program. He goes on to say how he and my mother "celebrated the realization," as every parent might, of their first child, continuing:

> . . . . *I learned just before we went to Washington in August '52. It was an exciting time (as much of our life was) and I was able to immerse myself into one of the most intellectual jobs I had*

had to date—the Plans Division of the Air Force! Little did I know that in less than a year I was to be appointed to the Strategic War Plans Committee of the Joint Chiefs of Staff and promoted to Colonel on my birthday in 1954.

You're probably wondering what this has to do with you. Well, it's this; your precious mother was such a trooper that I had no worries at home to distract me. You see, I could not discuss my work at home; there is no shop talk at that level. You were the topic of conversation.

Needless to say, I cherish the letter.

Fathers and mothers, write *real* letters to your children. Daughters and sons, I implore you to send handwritten notes to your loved ones. These material touchstones are more important than you can imagine.

The year was 1953. It served up Molotov cocktails of national security crises, among other weighty concerns.

My brother, Paul Jr., "DiDi," came the following year. Brother André, the next. We moved to Maxwell Air Force Base near Montgomery, Alabama, so Dad could attend the War College. But then the unthinkable happened. When I was three and DiDi, two, he drowned in a nearby irrigation ditch. I was taken to my grandparents' home in Charleston, South Carolina, for the aftermath and have no memory of this time. I do recall an earlier exchange, when DiDi asked me sweetly: "Whatcha doin'?" and I rebuffed him. It burns still.

Many years later, Mom was driving her now six children back home to Georgia, after visiting our great-grandparents in Andalusia, Alabama. She wanted to visit her little boy's resting place. In Montgomery, we found the cemetery and located the marker. Her suffering was compounded that day by the sad appearance of the neglected site. The stone, with its nearly life-size lamb, had sunk into the earth at an angle. I searched her face; it often expressed helplessness during those turbulent days of the late Sixties and early Seventies, but today it reflected an even deeper chagrin, if finally tempered by her usual, abiding resolve. She simply said, "Well, let's go," and, cranking the steering wheel of the station wagon, we continued on our way, my neck craning for one last, dispiriting view. She always maintained, "DiDi is one of the stars now." Far-removed from that mean grave.

Our sister, Gabrielle Evangeline, was born a month

Figure 5 The author at 4, at L'Aigle Noir Hotel in Fontainebleau in 1957

before DiDi died. She resembled an angel with her cherubic, curly white hair and perpetual look of eager surprise. Everything was a revelation. Named for Longfellow's lovers, Gabriel and Evangeline, the poet's inspiration was our Acadian ancestor, Louis Arceneaux, and his heartbroken love, Emmeline Labiche. The accounts differ, but artistic license has produced a poignant tale. We call our sister *Gabi,* or Bea. I pronounce *Gabi* with the second syllable accented, as spoken in France where we were stationed 1957-1961, and where I started school.

As Chief of the Atomic Plans Branch and Director of Operations of the Allied Air Forces of Central Europe, Dad was *very busy,* in retrospect. As children, we were clearly, or, naturally, oblivious. His office was located in a wing of the celebrated château in Fontainebleau. Originally a medieval hunting lodge, it was expanded and used by French royalty through the years. Before his exile, Napoleon Bonaparte bade farewell from its storied front steps to his troops. France was a member of NATO until 1966, when President de Gaulle withdrew from the organization. The country became a full member once again in 2008.

We rented a beautiful old home in the nearby village of Veneux-les-Sablons, named for its perfect glass-making sand. I attended school in the adjacent village, Moret-sur-Loing, known for the historic, riverside home of France's first Renaissance king, François I, 1494-1547. My brother and sisters and I played for hours in our large fenced

Figure 6 Gabi, André, Felicia with doll

yard, watched over by two venerable fir trees, and listening for the squeaking back gate and crunch of white gravel, telling us Daddy was home. André

Memory could, and would, bloom anew from *La Belle France,* the country of my heart. The gift of a second language and culture during one's formative years enlarges heart, mind, and soul. At least I hope so.

That first year brought a visit from Mama Ease, my paternal grandmother, and we made a trip to Grindelwald in the Swiss Alps. The very name and appearance of the village evoked a fairy tale, with an attending risk of danger. My father pointed out, through a telescope, the bivouacked climber who had died while scaling the rugged north face of the Eiger Peak. I can picture the dreadful image still, but cannot recall my reaction. The incident must have been explained in such a way as to mitigate horror, much as hearing a frightening bedtime story end peaceably—however disastrously for one of the characters. Either way, I fell in love with mountains, chalets and clanging goats and cows. Their bells and *mehs* made the only sound, save the wind whistling between peaks, and vast, green slopes changing to points of shining snow.

The following year, 1958, my parents took me to the World's Fair in Brussels. It was attended by forty million visitors during its several-month run. For my father, the trip may or may not have coincided militarily; I presume it did. My younger brother and sisters stayed home with responsible parties.

We toured international exhibits of the first major world exposition to be organized after WWII. The Atomium stands outside of Brussels. The famous architectural symbol of that fair is now a museum. Rising 335 feet above the fair, it was designed by engineer André Waterkeyn, in the shape of a unit cell of an iron crystal, magnified 165 billion times—the different spheres reached by escalators, stairs, and an elevator, house a restaurant and exhibits.

I gawked at replicas of the former Soviet Union's *Sputniks* I and II (meaning, "satellite"), the scientific and technological achievements rightly praised and on display. The future and the present had collided. The race was on. Meanwhile, MAD, or, "mutually assured destruction" reigned as deterrent, the atomic weapons poised as ghastly pawns on a chess board, half facing Western Europe, and half eastward toward the USSR in a horrifying gambit. The dangers were real and Santa Claus but a spirit. So far so good, and score everything for the spirit of goodness.

I didn't learn about this staggering arrangement until after the Soviet Union fell in 1991, when my father explained some of his responsibilities in France, those that had been declassified. The mind boggles.

Well, no wonder, I often mutter to myself.

SPRING II

Several years ago, in the stable, I discovered a grouping of five new (to me) mushrooms. They had jauntily popped up in the aisle beside the indoor hay. Luckily, they were easy to identify and I was thrilled. I'd found treasure. They were shaggy manes, *Coprimus comatus,* which happen to be a favorite wild mushroom in Russia, of all places. My, how their spores must fly! Diminutive ISBMs. (Tongue planted firmly in cheek.) These had not *deliquesced.* A delicious word meaning: to have self-consumed or decomposed. They turn black during this process and do not look appetizing at all. But these were perfect, not yet having flared their caps like an open umbrella. The shaggy mane refers to the wig-like appearance of the young top. They are delectable, sautéed in butter.

Mushrooms

Yes, yes, I know. *Huge* caveat here: **know your mushrooms**. Key them well. *If in doubt, leave it out,* as they say. Touch none you suspect to be poisonous. All this said, I mention those edible—and those dangerous—we have found on the place and nearby, with the strongest caution to check and double check your sources. A handy reference is *Mushrooms and Other Fungi, Black Hills,* by Gabel and Ebbert.

After a rain, creamy meadow mushrooms occasionally appear in the orchard, just below the hill near the water pump. Their gills are pinkish or brown;

pink when young, brown later—but still edible for a short time. They have a "skirt" or "veil" attached to the stem.

The *color* of the gills is the crux and identifier, as we also have Destroying Angels, from the genus *Amenita*. These are white, with *white* gills and a skirt or veil on the slender stem—which bulges, then tapers, where it grows from the soil. If you do touch them, wash soon with soap. We wear gloves and dispose of the poisonous varieties when we find them in the yard or orchard, just as other unwelcome critters are also shown the door, as it were. Those stories wait for another season.

In the woods behind the house, we've come across a large patch of fly agarics, the toadstools of Walt Disney fame, *Amanita muscaria*. Red tops with white dots. Pretty and poisonous. Leave them be. The best lesson is to show someone the specimen; second best is the photograph or drawing. Symptoms demand a trip to the clinic nine miles away, or a 911 call. The **National Poison Hotline** is **800-222-1222,** but rural living begs stocking an appropriate antidote. A slurry of activated charcoal (a teaspoon of the charcoal in four ounces of water) helps, but a stomach pump will probably be ordered anyway. An ounce of prevention?

Oyster mushrooms—those growing on trees—are edible. Found along creeks, on downed cottonwoods, like carbuncles gracing old ships or piers, we've gathered and fixed them for supper. But keying is key. Several varieties are simply too tough to eat. Puff balls are another delicious species, but only when young. Identify them first, as there are similar, less edible species. Cut into your find with a sharp knife. If it's still firm and white, it's fine.

Interesting to note, distinguish and enjoy, are the myriad subtle flavors of fungi, especially the wild ones.

Meadow mushrooms are classified the same family as the small white ones found in the grocer, and their taste is similar. Wetter niches in the Hills hide morels; we haven't yet experienced the pleasure. Returning to the house from a walk, I once discovered a boletus mushroom growing near the road and sautéed it for lunch.

Nearby Diversions to Counter *Ennui* or Cabin Fever

The final performances of the Matthews Opera House subscription series in Spearfish, an hour away, happen in spring. "Date night" may include dinner before the entertainment, always welcome, and both a treat. We decided that the Irish band, Socks in the Frying Pan, was the year's highlight, with Shakespeare's Othello coming in second, tying with the Portland Cello Project.

I mention the night out, one, to show you aren't completely without recourse when it comes to the occasional cultural event here in the back of beyond, and, two, that (for me) these diversions are as essential as they are entertaining. You might think this self-evident, but you'd be surprised how easy it is to grow inured to a certain day-in, day-out, nose-to-the-grindstone existence. My husband, case in point. He's part terrier, I'm convinced. Hence, tenacious (hence, my largely unconscious choice of a Jack Russell Terrier to present him years ago after a surgery—to lend cheer and certain comic relief). But yes, the incomparable Matthew's Opera House and their gallery in Spearfish, including the Festival in the Park they sponsor in July, are all bright, shiny opportunities for diversion and surprise.

Speaking of which, keep your eyes open. During an early spring trip to Spearfish, my eagle eye once spotted a trove of bushel baskets in a Safeway dumpster and I alerted Jeff. We came away with sixteen, most in good condition. For apple growers, a fortunate find.

So now we're dumpster divers . . . but we recycle. You could, too.

The garage stores "official" blue bags for glass, paper, tin cans, and plastic. A local church takes cans, and the rest is hauled to Rapid City, two hours away, tacked on to shopping trips or other business. We also keep a small scraps bucket in the kitchen pantry. It's destined for the compost bin located beside the large garden. (*No citrus or meat; fish is fine.*) Turn the whole mess with a pitchfork from time to time, then spread it on the soil when sufficiently decomposed. Rain provides the necessary moisture. "Give it back to the Earth" is pronounced from time to time. But remember, *no citrus.* It can arrest the process. Meat just invites critters.

You might wonder how date nights and recycling relate? They just do. All right; here's an image for you: we turn the compost pile to allow air and moisture to do their bit. Date nights, I suggest, are a turning over, with a proverbial pitchfork of communication and a subsequent airing. Not so wide a stretch if you think about it.

Further Spring Outdoor Chores: Planting and replanting

I required another two elderberries (making five in all), as I use the flowers and berries to make botanical tinctures and syrups. We ordered a pair, for cross-pollination (important for this variety), and Jeff planted them in the front yard. As with most young plants (and children), it's necessary to keep them regularly watered (nurtured) the first few years to encourage the roots (the sensibilities).

I pruned several dead stems in the older elderberry bushes, either caused by winter kill or age. Some winters are harsher than others, both *very* cold and snowy, but another may be "open," leading to a period of drought. Hans Christian Anderson wrote a fairy tale about The Elder Mother, or *Hylde Moer*. She wields power to protect, or to harm (we do not eat the berries uncooked). She demands respect and attention. The lore predicts a happy home where an elderberry grows, and the leaves may protect a person from evil when dried and hung near a doorway. It's polite to ask permission before harvesting flowers or berries—a simple matter of courtesy. Good luck may spring from the health the elderflower and berry promote.

- Amending garden soil: Jeff has discovered another source for manure. Because we no longer keep horses, chickens, or other livestock (for now, anyway), it's necessary to haul it, it just so happens, from the same neighbors who provide us with goat milk. Peat moss gives loft to the garden and is also (slightly) acidic. Our soil's pH is base, as mentioned, and there's a fair amount of bentonite clay, which is used in everything from binding agents to lipstick.
- *Dirt* and *soil* are not interchangeable. It has taken decades to build the garden soils and it should never be taken for granted. Soil organisms—the all-important microbes—are crucial to a healthy garden (and soils in general). We disrespect and ignore soil and

microbes at our peril. When I say our, I mean Earth's. It is (we are) all related. Truly.

- The rain gauge resumes its post (on a post) in spring, so we can measure moisture. How else will I know when to begin hand-watering my trees? (My trees to water, I mean.) The weather remains a common topic of conversation here in these Hills—*how much rain one has received*. The banter is as relevant and beneficial as the rain itself.

- We plant the gardens after danger of frost is past and when the soil has warmed enough. Reminder: the official date is May 15, but this is changing. In all fairness, Jeff does most of the planting. I give him a hand (in all fairness). Our farmer marketing is limited to garlic, grapes, shallots, and apples, depending on the year. I've suggested we *could* plant less, as there are only the two of us. Weighing the contribution of fresh fruit and vegetables to our community factors in, and a sense of satisfaction prevails.

- An up-keep expense that chafes is the purchase of gravel for our third-of-a-mile stretch of dirt road to the highway. I've occasionally, no, *often* opined that we could have had the lane tarred by now for the money. A moot argument. Jeff insists a tar road requires maintenance as well, so. . . . He spreads the dump-truck loads of gravel with the tractor, and the road must be "crowned" from time to time too, to keep it properly, *civilly* engineered (allowing for drainage, and to improve the surface).

- Every other spring or so, the front porch benefits from being stained. Not an onerous chore, the two of us can complete it in a couple of hours and *poof!* the area looks tended once more. The house itself was repainted in 2013, and may not need a new coat for another fifteen years, barring a *hell*acious hailstorm, which can happen. (See Summer.)

Figure 7 Garbling lemon balm for teas and tinctures

OF CHAMPIONS AND A FRENCH *NOUNOU*

I n a *A Singular Notion,* I described how a certain forest in France filled me with awe and peace. Children will seek out solace and acceptance, if unconsciously. Surrounding Fontainebleau is the first designated "national forest" of France, where kings and courtiers once hunted for boar and stag. The beasts yet range.

In November of 1959, just before her sixteenth birthday, our new nanny (*nounou* in French) arrived. She had grown up not far from the great forest and, like a younger, very French, Mary Poppins, she'd shown up, primarily (I believe), to ease my siblings' and my sense of upheaval and loss, however miniscule in comparison to our parents'. I say *new* nanny, for Micheline Pommeret was number three, after Babette and Vivienne.

My mother was distraught much of the time, and clearly mourning her lost son—a tragic fact I only realized years after her own death in 2000. She had a talent for make-believe, however; a glorious aptitude, and not the malicious brand. Mom could beam for a photograph at the drop of a hat, as they say, and she demonstrated what her Sisters of Charity nursing instructors called *intestinal fortitude.* The strength of her personality lay in her formidable sense of duty. She was, after all, an Air Force spouse. But in several photographs taken in France—scanned and emailed by a thoughtful sister—my mother's grief-stricken expression, unguarded, is all-too evident.

Reminded of my own prior easy cheerfulness and capacity for delight (evidenced by earlier pictures), I too had fallen more and more introspective and circumspect. Emotions are all too infectious. By seven years of age, I'd grown fairly solemn.

Micheline boarded with us during the week, returned to her family on weekends. Mom wasn't without recourse during the day. Other officers' wives provided support—if they were cognizant of Paul and Millie Latiolais' tragic loss. Sensitive matters tended to precede one's arrival at a new military base, given *l'esprit de corps* of the times. The women would organize junkets to Paris, thirty minutes away, or take road trips to shop in the Netherlands; once, for an entire battery of yellow porcelain enamel kitchen ware.

Privileged to travel alone with my mother on occasion, tucked into the fire engine red, MGA roadster, I experienced a different side of her thirty-year-old self on those trips—free of burdens, and curious as to what lay beyond the plane tree-shaded turns. I cherish the memories. I could relax my own vigilance, if this is what it was. We were adventurers and she was the brave one; her defining quality was that of courage, or *guts*, as Dad would say.

I could understand and speak the language well enough by then, if the childish version, but I'd grown timid. Mom's "kitchen French" sufficed most of the time. Once, we were stopped by a patrolman, for speeding I suspect, and she feigned misunderstanding. I piped up that I knew what the man was saying, while she tried to shush me with one of her looks. The man gave her a warning, but knew he'd been bamboozled.

We motored to Pisa, Florence, Rome, and north into Germany. I remember her asking a road-weary me, six years old, if I wanted to see an Ice Capades, having spotted the advertisement as we passed. Ambivalent even then, I finally agreed. How surprised and rapt I was, my arms dangling over the railing near our table, as I watched the skaters perform near-magical feats, as close to flying as I could imagine. The lights, colors, and sheer exuberance of the dancers transported me to a heaven of ineffable joy.

We may well draw strength to continue plodding through a personal hell by living through our children, and borrowing their enthusiasms. How we beamed, my mother and I. Her smile was sincere. I know it was. No Disneyland could have compared with these travels—the superior experience, in my view. I never visited Disney World until I was thirty-six, with my children, but I did make the acquaintance of a certain talking rodent while in France. . . .

Having no television, our parents received their news via the small radio in the den. It may have been the BBC; I recall it broadcast in English. Perhaps Voice of America. However, our neighbor, Monsieur Alexandre Chèvrier, owned a TV set. He and his wife were elderly, with pendulous ears and a twinkle in their eye. Monsieur was bald and always dressed impeccably in black suit, vest, white shirt, and narrow black tie.

One day I was summoned to watch the Mickey Mouse Club with him, and this is where I might have acquired a taste for champagne. Monsieur Chèvrier would pour me a small liqueur glass of the bubbly and pass me several ladyfingers to dunk into the golden liquid. What's not to like? The perfectly married flavors and the sensation of sucking the wine through the lightly sweet cookie approach the *Madeleines* of Proust memory. I do not recall confessing this treat to my parents, somehow guessing its unorthodox nature. On the U.S.S. United States, during our initial Atlantic crossing, my little brother André and I sampled the port wine as my father lay seasick and semi-conscious in bed. Mom was walking the deck for some air with baby Gabi. I don't recall this naughtiness, but it provided a chuckle through the telling much later.

Our old neighbor and I laughed at Mickey's antics. I'll bet we did. . . .

Monsieur Chèvrier's gardener, Léon, was our friend. He dressed in laborer's denim (de Nîmes) jeans, chambray shirt, black beret, and gum boots. His smile could break your heart and his ruddy complexion was a roadmap of capillaries. *"Monsieur le Colonel,"* he addressed my father, until begged to call him, simply, Paul. During WWII, Léon had spent several months in a German concentration camp. He adored my parents and offered to help any way he could with the yard work, despite his own garden and orchard to tend next door. When he could escape the office and home fires for a day or two, my father, in return for his kindness, invited him on hunts. They brought home braces of pheasants, ducks or rabbits; once, a haunch of wild boar (the beast divided among the hunters). Julienne, our housekeeper, patiently taught Mom how to prepare them all.

These lessons might have encouraged her to join a cooking class in Paris at *Le Cordon Bleu*. French cuisine became her particular brand of magic, her practice, and a brilliant passion. I believe it saved her. Judging from my own choice of diversion (writing), and its salubrious effects, anything we put our heart and soul into is bound to proclaim, "Get thee behind me!" to *any* version of adversary present.

Mom never suffered fools. Have I mentioned this? But she needed *cuisine* as her champion.

During our four years in France, she made several life-long friends. Once, she and Anne, the wife of a jovial officer we children called Uncle Noël, drove to Germany. On their way back, a driver in a VW Bug swerved into their lane and smashed into them, head-on. It was dark and raining, and the man in the VW was instantly killed. Mom, then seven months pregnant with our sister Felicia, was driving, and the station wagon's steering wheel jammed into her swollen stomach, the glass from the shattered windshield spraying both her and Anne.

I would walk to and from the convent school, about a half-mile away, often in the company of an older neighbor girl, Michelle, but alone on occasion. That afternoon, I remember climbing the kitchen steps and opening the door to my mother for the first time since she'd returned from the hospital. She was sitting on one of the kitchen chairs, a blanket, I think, around her shoulders—it could have been a robe—and my eyes flew to her face, crisscrossed with ugly black stitches on nearly every square inch. It was horrendous. I don't recall my initial reaction, but the image is seared into my mind. She was stoic and worked hard to put me at ease. My father, sitting beside her, helped me to understand, with soothing words and reassurance.

Oddly enough, I beheld him in similar state years later, also due to an automobile accident, though with not as many cuts. Ten short years separate the two events, yet, how many ligatures might have been required to bind the invisible cuts both parents had suffered, and would endure?

Figure 8 Veneux-les-Sablons, 1961: from left, Renée, Gabi, Mom and Nancy, André, his hand on Felicia's shoulder, and Alexandria.

SPRING III

*"You have to be a romantic to invest yourself,
your money and your time in cheese."*
                                    ~Anthony Bourdain

Springtime brings tax prep—as well as blizzards. Wyoming exacts no state income tax (*yet*), but the IRS demands its share and we oblige, for the privilege of living in the country. I wish I could say my husband and I are amazingly well-organized, and that every receipt is efficiently filed away. It's not one of my talents. I normally do the monthly bookkeeping, but the yearly tax tedium falls to Jeff. Even when he sends his tallies off to be figured, it's still a hectic project. But this isn't a treatise on personal finances, so I'll leave you to your own devices. I note the chore only to show that tedious interruptions can, and will, disrupt the more fragrantly-oiled machine of routine.

Housework—*the usual suspects*—I omit, as everyone has their preferences. A long-time friend insists she cleans her bathroom bi-annually, whether it needs it or not. I can never tell if she's joking and dare not ask.

A few considerations outside of the usual:
- Watering plants in the house and studio/atrium, if you choose to keep them: self-explanatory. We like to use the rainwater collected in the large tub below the downspout near the back porch. In winter we'll fill five-gallon buckets with snow and let it melt in the fifty-degree studio/atrium.

If one of us is working for a period, a portable heater eases the chill. Jeff carves in the room, and I house my sound system there. One day I may return to painting—the translucent ceiling floods the space with good light.

- If you travel at all during quieter winter months (they're all quiet here), or even over a few days, plants and animals need to be tended—an important but obvious concern made plain in Scott and Helen Nearing's seminal book, *Living the Good Life,* advocating why they avoided livestock and stuck to crops, in favor of simplicity.

Figure 9 "Woman" by Jeff

- Read/write/make music and art/cook/bake/tinker (read: "strengthen the things which remain"), and, when it's available, make goat cheese with the neighbor's milk, a new venture and one I enjoy, because we *love* goat cheese. Occasionally it's gamey, but most of the time delicious.

Jeff turns to his wood carving and spy thrillers, and catches up with friends and family by phone or text.

I love a quote by Annie Dillard, "How we spend our days is, of course, how we spend our lives."

In concert with nurturing relationships with our children and grandchildren, extended family, friends and the community these ordinary, daily (redundant, for clarity) activities compose The Stuff of Life. You may question the inclusion of hobbies (dreadful word, but there it is; I prefer "passions," but I strive to be clear, so—*hobbies*). Work is work in the end, to *expend energy* for gain or profit in return. Physics plus passion equals fulfillment. These necessarily cross seasonal boundaries. And, as time permits, I *make* time for the reading, writing, music, cooking, baking, and making of goat cheese, some of which are hobbies, and others, animating principles.

Having no basement to store foodstuffs requiring cooler temperatures, we dug a root cellar. Below the house, it's off the terrace path leading to my study. The topography allowed for the traditional cave (of sorts), and a friend brought over his backhoe. We acquired two sections of a septic tank (never used!) to plant into the side of the hill, and then covered it with soil. It now resembles a fairy hill from a distance. (No one else thinks so, however. Some suggest "a porcupine," for the tall, quill-like grasses growing on top.)

We lined the necessary ante-chamber (leading into the cellar) with railway ties, and for several years—even after it was painted—I forbade apples to be stored in the cellar, as they were absorbing the smell (and so, taste) of the creosote preservative. This, sadly, is still the case. I sit here munching on one of the apples, stored since October as an experiment. In mid-winter, they should taste as close to "just-picked" as possible. (Refrigeration diminishes flavor, I find, so the studio serves for now, its indoor temperature set at a cooler temperature.)

Jeff spent much time and energy building splendid Williams-Sonoma-like shelving units for the cellar, employing their catalogue as a guide, I remember. This man is handy *and* frugal, a trait he inherited from a mother who grew up on an Arkansas farm during The Depression.

Most of the shelves are now stocked with homemade wine or cordials from our grapes and fruit. As mentioned, the *labrusca* variety has proven unsuitable, but what to do with bottles and bottles of the aging stuff? *Wait,* I hear. You never know. Meanwhile, we have cleared out boxes and boxes of empty wine bottles, some given to us by wine-drinking friends, to open space for garden storage. A bushel of potatoes and several buttercup squashes keep well enough and seem to escape the creosote curse.

The cellar stays cool on hot days. Humidity is important, but not too much, and above ground (on the "porcupine's" back) an air duct may be adjusted to remove moisture. Close it for winter. Opening the doors on occasion will air the space, but it may invite mice or snakes. Beware!

The cellar would make a great hiding place for a game of hide-and-seek, but you might get chilly. We installed a light. We could hang a corkscrew for the adults, off the shelves. Add a bistro table and two small chairs. We could.

Making *Chèvre*, or Goat Cheese

When I learned a neighbor raised dairy goats (and by *neighbor,* I mean someone within a ten-mile radius), I perked up. Bonnie Jo and her husband Zack, a boot maker and rancher, keep goats, sheep and horses, dogs and probably cats—though I never see any when I enter their yard. They're raising their children to care for the animals and to carry on The Life. Bonnie Jo was a classmate of our son and married into one of the ranching families north of us.

She is duly proud of her nannies and their creamy white milk. As entrepreneur of all things goat-y, her business card reads *Goats Gone Wild.* Jeff and I drove up one day last fall to meet the ladies. Apart from a billy's own promiscuous proclivities, I had read that keeping one in too-close proximity can cause nannies to exude a hormone that will taint their milk. But the old goat (who probably wasn't all that old) was penned at a distance while dozens of nannies and their babies freely roamed.

Kid goats coax a smile and bring joy. They are that funny. The true comedians of the barnyard.

Bonnie Jo showed us the shed where she milked. She apparently doesn't need a stanchion, but seated on a stool, she merely ties the goat and *goes a-milkin'*. It occurred to me that each of us honors our passions and preferences in some way. My mind boggles at the prospect of having to milk so many animals twice a day. (That I can sit for hours on end, tapping on a keyboard, would likely draw a similar response from Bonnie Jo.) I am thankful that Jeff and I can simply drive up and buy a gallon or a half, though a couple of times the muddy ruts to their place, snaking down into a back-country valley, have left us wide-eyed.

For a nominal fee, she offered to demonstrate her favorite cheese-making method and we agreed. We were the luckier ones who took home samples of goat lotion, soap, and lip balm. Bonnie Jo uses apple cider vinegar instead of rennet to culture a ricotta-like soft cheese. I hoped to make something similar to the *chèvre,* sold in short logs, that I've bought at the grocer.

After watching a video on the process, I ordered liquid rennet and a packet of *chèvre* culture, a powder that must be kept in the freezer, and something called "butter cloth," its weave tighter than cheesecloth. Bonnie Jo had lent me a book on the art of cheesemaking, and there I found my working recipe. It's remarkably simple, though all rests on temperature, humidity, and attention, three factors that can prove tricky. The goat farmer in the video cautioned her viewers to stir in the culture delicately and, later, to separate the curds with *great* care when placing them into the butter cloth-lined strainer.

I was rewarded with four well-formed creamy logs. They smelled divine—always a good sign. I wind up with a quart of whey, more or less, for each half gallon of milk. Goat milk has more protein content than cow milk. I mix whey with my muesli overnight for a tangy cereal.

After working in a bit of salt (for both flavor and as preservative) the new cheese is then ready to age, and placed in a container for the purpose (on a slotted tray, to hold the cheese above any whey that may still drip out). The root cellar is perfect for this. The cheese should be turned daily, but if you miss a day, no worries. After a week (or longer, if you're patient), the logs may be rolled in herbs or chopped nuts, or mixed with sweetened, chopped dried cranberries—a treat—or left *au naturel,* how we enjoy it. It is mouth-watering on French bread with a half-teaspoon of fig preserves.

So far, I've only had to return two batches to the Earth for being too strong, gamey, or tainted—take your pick. Once, I suspected the milk had been stored long in the fridge and its acid content prevented the culture from working properly. Another time, the smell interfered with our sensibilities. (This is not understated.) Bonnie Jo explained that occasionally, in the spring, the nannies' milk can taste strong.

I take the good with the bad. It is a satisfying venture and, one day, I may keep a couple of nannies, but for now, owing to travel, I'll more than appreciate and make do with an intrepid neighbor whose nannies can furnish the amazing liquid.

Figure 10 Separating goat cheese (chèvre) from the whey

Meanwhile. . . .

• The electric water heater is in the storeroom on the back porch, where it smartly keeps the contents of the room from freezing. Keep an extra heating element on hand, in case. The odds predict it will "naturally" go out on a Sunday. If you're prepared, it will *always* choose another day. This is elementary physics. Or some similar logic.

• Replace furnace filters every six months, spring and fall. Size 16x20x1. Record dates and post a reminder for the next change in plain sight.

• *Reverse Osmosis* sounds like a magic trick and in a way it is. But we've come to prefer the taste it imparts to our water, or non-taste, as it were. Many of the chemicals are removed; it's conditioned water, and filtered. (When we moved in, and for several years after, the hard water left rust-colored rings in bathtub and made for dingy white laundry. Even our hair took it up!) The technician appears from Western Water Conditioning in Gillette once a year in spring to replace the machine's filters (located under the kitchen sink). He tests it—and the water softener—in the back porch storeroom.

• Hot tub maintenance: we made the purchase two decades ago with Jeff's chronic back pain in mind. (Regrettably, the third surgery was not the charm. He was told he must Pay Attention to keep from re-injury and has now recovered. His wife's nagging prevents nothing, nor does it improve the odds.)

We enjoy the soothing hydrotherapy (and the hot water lowers blood pressure, to cite another medicinal value). The tub requires once or twice-yearly emptying, cleaning, and refilling, and routine checks for balanced chemicals, depending on its use. The kit is kept in the storeroom with instructions. Take a sample of the outside hose water (not softened) to the Hot Tub man in Spearfish and he will tell you exactly how much of what to use.

Our croft's "water feature" provides a restful, peaceful dimension, as the spa sits on the covered back porch in view of a forested slope, the Dalgo crab apple tree, the Witch's Garden, and a statue of the serene Buddha. From a low ponderosa limb hangs the source of a deep, resounding tone, a perfect Zen reminder. Created from a three-foot-long former oxygen tank, the bell's nine-inch-wide tin fan catches the breeze, to knock the round wooden clapper against the hollow steel. At night, I hear it as a ship's signal.

THE QUIET GRACE OF A BLANK PAGE

In Japan, *shinrin-yoku,* or forest bathing, is the practice of engaging your five senses while passing time in a wooded setting. It is "most beneficial," declares the author of *Forest Bathing, How Trees Can Help You Find Health and Happiness.* Dr. Qing Li is also the chairman of the Japanese Society for Forest Medicine. The pairing rings true to my ears. Like a bell hung in a forest.

Figure 11 Jeff, Soaking

Today I am writing—and steeping—in a lodgepole forest on Casper Mountain, in the near center of Wyoming, at our family cabin. More a hut, given its size, but cozy. It's "dry," meaning: no running water. From the porch, I hear and feel the wind's *shhhhh* through the trees—like ocean waves. More than at home, here the strong, bright smell of pine and musty decayed matter, *duff,* infuses all. The mountain air is sharp to the nose, due to little moisture, save after a rain. My eyes drink beauty, if subject to an occasional, dry-wind irritation. I sense a profound belonging, even while perceiving through a wild and wooly vision.

Whether soaking in hot water, or bathing in forest air, the elements of nature, within and without, conspire to heal whatever ails. Through heat of a crackling wood fire, a warming wool lap blanket, and the taste of a warm cup of cocoa, I allow for consciousness to settle. Like the piney forest after a wind storm, I finally sense no separation. It is good to just be and permit the blank page now and then. . . .

SPRING IV

To claim good fortune may prompt an adverse response. Best to simply feel and express gratitude. For innumerable reasons. To wit, after the water well gave up back in 2010, complications ensued and we required an altogether whole new hole drilled. A permit from the state is required to drill, and this raised the opportunity for Wyoming's low population and friendly neighbors to shine (even if from the adjacent town). Jeff wasn't sure how we would manage without water. A friend was able to push the permit, likely on account of my having just undergone open-heart surgery. *Thank you, Ralph.*

"Artesian," the driller declared with a grin, and the water is much less hard than that from the original aquifer—which also happened to lie deeper underground. It's important to do yearly softener and water checks. (Incidentally, we store several gallons of drinking water in the kitchen pantry, just in case. I'll discuss the generator later. Another "in case".)

Speaking of checkups, spring's a good time of year to schedule physicals, after you've received your lab results from the county blood draw, which is regularly scheduled in April. For $35 (as of this writing) you can order a battery of basic lab tests performed to present to your doctor, at a fraction of the cost of having it done by a clinic or independent laboratory.

The health care question vis-à-vis living rurally raises another subject, one that demands a certain amount of self-care and mindfulness—both of which, from time to time, suffer from life's surprises. I am keenly grateful for the care and expertise I received before, during and after the heart surgery, with family and friends given equal thanks with doctors and nurses. I thank the EMTs and ambulance service in Hulett, after a second "event" required a quick ride to Rapid City. Everyone was prompt and competent. I mention this emergency to allay possible concerns in that regard. Too, four hours north in Billings, Mayo Clinic has joined that city's healthcare services. *Flight for Life* helicopters stand ready, if necessary.

My interest in herbal medicine and traditional remedies stem from an over-romanticized notion of medieval and pioneer life, and I've enjoyed plant study (such as it was) since I was young. You may remember the film, *Green Mansions,* with Audrey Hepburn and Anthony Perkins. I don't recall how old I was. Ten? Eleven? But it moved me, despite its less than positive reviews. Mixed with the forest of Fontainebleau and the Alps, an alchemy served to wake up a dormant disposition toward the natural world and her gifts, never mind her dangers—i.e., rattlesnakes. The *ouroboros* symbol as yin/yang: we might learn to finally expect opposites and understand wholeness as accepting, and incorporating, all. The symbol depicts a snake eating its own tail, signifying infinity and eternal cycles. This brings me to the next section. . . .

On Critters and Varmints

If you stroll the perimeter of the yard and orchard, note the high fencing. Strung eighteen inches along the outside, the same distance off the ground, you will also notice (we hope) an electric line. This dissuades the deer. They love apples, you see. We toss them quite a few windfalls over the course of a season, which may not prove the most compassionate tack, as it could serve to increase their appetite. We do it anyway. The electric line is the secret, we've found, as deer are remarkable at bounding over obstacles. The electric shock isn't terrible, but does gain their attention and takes only once. Unfortunately, this stinging solution does not work against raccoons, badgers, rabbits, voles, packrats and snakes—notably, the venomous sort.

Jeff hauls out the live trap most years to catch a critter and remove it to a distant field, up the highway. This mainly works with raccoons. (A larger breed of dog deters their trespassing today, but not entirely.) We mostly ignore the rabbits, as they haven't seemed to bother much—there being so much forage. I enjoy spotting the sweet cottontails in the yard. Their mating behavior is not to be missed, as they hop straight up in the air from a standstill, like Mexican jumping beans.

Eddy the terrier was an excellent ratter in the past, but age slowed her down, so Jeff runs a mousetrap line year-round. An herbal remedy called Fresh CAB Botanical Rodent Repellent is somewhat effective. We place traps and/or CAB in the sunroom studio, garage, shop, pantry and storeroom. If traps are not checked regularly, you will know by the stench.

Rattlesnakes and badgers require the more cautious and draconian approach. I've been known to patrol the area, especially when children are expected or present. The kids are lectured, not to cause fear (well, maybe a little) but to teach them respect. The snakes are most dangerous in the fall during molt, when blindness causes them to strike at anything. Badgers will attack with no provocation, the wicked wee beasties. Neither are welcome, but I've yet to compose a snake/badger satire to entice them to leave us alone.

And yes, Virginia, there are snakes in the garden.

One day, as I was contentedly picking raspberries, I glanced toward the tomato plants five feet away to see a three-foot rattler devouring a squirrel, its bushy tail emerging from the locked jaws of said snake. My guts turned to soup. At least it was in no position to strike at me.

These stories are not meant to horrify or detract, but to educate and warn. Over the thirty-plus years we've lived on this land, we've encountered fewer than twenty snakes in the yard and orchard. Twenty too many. It's a good idea to mow and stick to established paths, or the road, when hiking anytime but winter, when a hard freeze chases them into their holes. At the very least, wear high boots and long pants. Jeff has taken to occasionally carrying a .22 with bird shot. The prevailing advice: *never* put your hand where you can't see it; or feet, for that matter, whenever weeding or gathering strawberries.

Our county boasts two turkey seasons: spring and autumn. In spring, it falls in May. Only gobblers may be taken in the spring, as the hens are preparing hatches. No threat from us any longer, we do anticipate the yearly hunting trip of long-time friends who drive over from Powell, across the state. The house party is a highlight of mid-spring. Kim and Jon stop at Costco in Billings, to pick up all manner of exotic (to us) eatables and libations. Most years, Jon fills his license, but when he doesn't, no regrets, as we savor our time together.

These are "deep" visits, as only a house party can be. Kim and I plunge into topics and, being like-minded, we generally arrive at similar conclusions, but she's the more astute when it comes to emotional intelligence. Kim can recognize a harebrained attitude like no other, and is willing to say. I find these kinds of friends are your better angels. We'd all be wiser to heed, or at least consider carefully, their observations and/or course corrections. Friends as . . . . navigators.

Figure 12 Jon McDowell, Jeff, and Gabe, Turkey Hunting

A WORLD OF POSSIBLE

Metaphor mollifies, certainly, but also elucidates. More often than not, my parents' private hell over the loss of their child was mitigated by its opposite: an unbounded joy, true *joie de vivre,* in most extraordinary fashion, and they carried on. I started to say, "They knew *how* to carry on," but this is not accurate. They simply soldiered on, bravely at times and at others—as numb, wounded warriors falling out of line. Never, thankfully, at the same time.

Their own better angels knew. *Knew what?* you ask. That they had six children to bring up.

Figure 13 Preparing to leave France, 1961, Micheline on right.

Perhaps due to the car accident, my sister was born shaking her head, a continuous *unh-unh*. Brain damage was feared, but in time the shaking ceased and she fell in gloriously with the rest of us. At this writing, Felicia is the first of us to undergo cancer treatment and double strokes. Our *sweetest* sister retains her cheerful disposition, when the triple insult might have soured anyone else.

Alexandria (Alex) was born a year later, while Dad was away in Norway on military assignment. I thought she resembled a Madame Alexander doll, her features perfectly drawn, with eyes like stars. Mom bore seven children in eight years. Nancy arrived last and was three months old in 1961 when we all boarded a TWA transatlantic flight back to the States. Gabi and I wore matching dresses; André looked smart in his shorts suit and bowtie; Felicia and Alex endured starched organdy dresses; and Nancy was decked in near-baptismal splendor. The poodles, Inki and Chi Chi (bred), crossed the Atlantic in the aircraft luggage compartment.

The flight must have seemed an eternity for our parents, for us, for the other passengers and for the pets—especially the pets.

Stateside, Dad drove ahead in the MG with André, leaving Mom to take us from New York City to Richmond, Virginia, where Aunt Lucille and her large, loving, and rambunctious family lived. Once there, Chi Chi promptly gave birth to a litter of black and chocolate puppies. After giving both us broods time to adjust, we climbed back into the station wagon—dogs in the rear— and continued to the North Carolina air base. We kept one of the chocolate puppies and named him Brutus— whether for the Roman senator, or Popeye's nemesis, I don't know. Authentic French poodles quickly found homes.

Nine years before, in 1952, Nurse Millie Blackburn and Lt. Col. Paul Latiolais ("Latch" to colleagues) met in New Orleans' VA Hospital, where his brother Bobby was being treated for cancer. Mom experienced a *coup de foudre,* as they say in France. A thunderclap. She broke her engagement to an established physician and married my father less than three months after their first date. The Air Force pilot was evidently not "through with women," as he had written to his mother in 1946 or '47. His first wife had left him when he was stationed in Japan during the Occupation after WWII. Then had come Korea, where he served as Director of Combat Operations for the Fifth Air Force for six months. In December of 1950, the Air Force ordered him to Hollywood for a year-long temporary duty as technical advisor for the Robert Mitchum-Ann Blyth "romantic war film," *One Minute to Zero.*

Mom was an Alabama red-dirt girl and far removed from Hollywood glitter and intrigue, but given the post-war culture of the time, I daresay the officer cut a glamorous figure, with his stories of moviemaking *and* flying in two wars. The real deal. He exuded a natural charm (helpful in star circles, I suspect). They were married in a civil ceremony with her jazz-singing girlfriend as one of the witnesses. Having converted to Catholicism after entering Charity Nursing School, Mom's affiliation was to be short-lived, but only in terms of formality. My Catholic father's divorce was grounds for *excommunication.* An appalling word. Coupled with courage, Mom's faith, the purely generic kind, preserved our family.

Theirs was a marriage *for the books,* as they say. Passionate, volatile, devoted, and true. It hit all the major chords, with several minor passages thrown in for good measure and, lest I be coaxed to explain, I ask only,

"What makes any marriage?"—much as I might wonder what constitutes a moving symphony. The movements, resolution and denouement. And then, the silence. I recount her demise in my earlier collection, *A Singular Notion*. After Mom's passing, my father survived for four years. "Lived" may be a stretch.

In her teen years, her father, Hiram Blackburn, a WWI Navy vet known as "Jack," moved his family to Charleston Heights, South Carolina, to work at the Naval Yard as ship's carpenter. After high school, Mom and her sister joined the work force, neither choosing to teach, a woman's traditional career. Glamorous Aunt Avis became a TWA airline *stewardess,* as they were then called, while mostly-practical Mom chose nursing school. Veritable Dashwood sisters, Marianne and Elinor. Our maternal grandmother was a seamstress, though "tailor" is more apt. One day, she would replicate Mom's *haute couture* dresses, by visually *borrowing* the pattern. I called my grandmother *MonMon*, pronounced with the nasalized French "*on*," the n silent. My siblings would call her MoMo, and I use this spelling hereafter.

Uncle Bobby did not survive the stomach cancer and Dad was devastated. His older brother had been a father-figure. I suspect the death ushered further painful memories for him whose own father, almost a quarter-century before, had languished in the New Orleans Baptist Hospital for a time. Grandfather died, ultimately, from a bladder infection, after being shot at close range with a sawed-off shotgun. At least this was the story I was told.

Felix M. Latiolais was serving as the first sheriff of Lafayette Parish, Louisiana, when Dad was born in 1920. In a disturbing anecdote, repeated solely for sociological significance, it was conveyed to me that my grandmother took young Paul and Bobby to the

Lafayette hospital shortly after their father had been shot. She then instructed both boys to put their hands, "in the hole a black man made." I don't know what the boys did, or if the provocative demand was made for effect, but my father, of gentler sensibilities, taught his own children to be color blind. He never discussed the matter and I never asked about it. A trusted friend, who often sat by and listened to Dad's stories, added that, after he was shot, my grandfather ordered no one touch the man, fearing a mob. The account I was taught, first related to my father as a small boy, was intended to mitigate heartbreak, no doubt.

In preparing this section, I researched a fuller version of the incident. As mentioned earlier, my sister Felicia contends with the effects of a double stroke. The past is her bailiwick, I've always thought, and history her "happy place." She is our family genealogist and on a recent visit with her, after much excited "discussion" and motioning, she plucked from her prodigious archives a file. The Louisiana newspaper clippings dating from 1922 included the testimony of the "negro," Emile Hebert. I read that he and his wife, with infant, were returning from a family visit, when they encountered three men, including the sheriff (unbeknownst to him) on a muddy road, a usual occurrence in those times and climate, I suspect. Mr. Hebert requested right of way where my grandfather and his two companions were standing; they had just returned from procuring a shovel to free their vehicle mired in a mudhole.

"Why are you whistling?" one of them asked the rig's driver. He responded that he'd only been whistling at his horse (a common encouragement to coax one over nasty terrain, though this could be misinterpreted). Someone then threw a stone at Mr. Hebert—its size and thrower not identified. What followed could be relegated to tragic misadventure and/or misfortune. I *want* to say, "abject stupidity on the part of all parties," but it's hardly my call. Mr. Hebert then reached down, pulled a shotgun from the buckboard and fired twice. One in the sheriff's party now lay dead. Swinging the shovel to intervene, the sheriff missed his mark and wound up hitting the man's wife and baby, knocking them off their wagon. It rolled over them, resulting, miraculously, in no injury to mother or child, due to the mud, I presume. Mr. Hebert quickly reloaded and fired again, hitting my grandfather in the side and simultaneously wounding the second man. The article concludes, "The negro says that he continued on his way home where he was found by the posse, and arrested with his brother, Mazard Hebert. The negro's wife and brother have been rushed away to another jail." No explanation followed about the brother's role.

After a hospital stay, Grandfather was eventually returned to his home to recover.

Pneumonia led to complications, including infection, but he was eventually able to return to work, now as night Chief of Police, moonlighting at a motor vehicle company. In 1924, his assailant was acquitted in a mistrial. "The jury after deliberating all night was unable to agree." Family lore suggests the man was lynched. I pray this was not the case, but a separate newspaper article, dating from the same era, actually reported when a "lynching" was to take place.

My grandparents may have held differing worldviews.

Grandfather Felix was only fifty years old at his death three years later, a bladder infection cited as cause. Mama Ease (Louise) was hired as a clerk in the courthouse and continued to raise their many children. She bravely nurtured my father's passion in airplanes, once handing over a tidy sum (during The Depression) so he could buy a short ride in a travelling barnstormer's bi-plane. Dad wrote poignantly about the incident in his aviation memoir.

His big brother Bobby and sister Lucille also encouraged him. Dad left his manuscript unfinished, but dedicated, *"To all youngsters, who would fulfill their dreams."* After he passed away in 2004, I took it up, adding photos and material written about him, to publish it in 2010 as a short run.

Curiously, our great-grandfather on our mother's side, John "Mace" Blackburn, also served as a sheriff. He disappeared altogether, never to be found. While Dad was quick and willing to share family histories, Mom was reticent. I regret not asking her to share more of her stories.

I touch on my parents' and grandparents' lives as one might prepare soil to dig more easily, say, when transplanting a beloved flower; in this case, through time, to illustrate how our roots may serve as foundation, ballast, and a force. While it's not strictly necessary to be aware of stories that *explain* us to ourselves, a rudimentary understanding of one's childhood—even in retrospect and hindsight—may be gained from the memory, imagined or real, of a sturdy grounding (the Earth ever resting firmly beneath us), never mind the sometime-knotted mass of circumstances.

A plant, a tree—or a child—absorbs nutrients and vital moisture from their roots. They *"fix"* or *establish* the herb—or, the person—I daresay. Establish and acknowledge when, and where, you were perfectly content and deeply nourished. Create an "anchor" of the memory, a root, in order to revisit it. My anchor-roots include memories, cherished gifts, photographs, music—and never least, my loved ones. They serve to antidote more adverse experience.

One such memory (that explains myself to myself) involves a horse and carriage ride with my mother. A winding road among dark fir trees, the clip-clop and squeaking of the harness the only sounds I recall. The wind may have been blowing in the tree tops, and the driver may have clucked encouragement to the animal. I'm certain the horse blew a few times from the exertion.

Arriving at our destination, I was handed down to the ground after my mother by the driver, near the entrance of a castle. Neuschwanstein Castle in southern Bavaria is Disneyland's model for its main attraction, Sleeping Beauty's castle. I was six or seven, and when I was young and impressionable, I was young and impressionable. The Disney film was my second favorite *after* Peter Pan, being the consummate tom-boy.

The castle interior is largely lost to me; the imposing outdoor asymmetries and turrets I do recall—and, the possibility of fairy tales being real. Here was proof in stone: "Swan-stone," in the German. Its builder, King Ludwig II, was declared insane for his lavish expenditures (not solely on this castle). This assessment is under review. He was clearly a romantic and died under suspicious circumstances.

A detailed painting of Neuschwanstein hangs in our home, a gift from an Air Force general and his wife. When we first returned to the States in 1961, I happened to notice the image in their quarters at Pope Air Force Base in North Carolina, grandly exhibited above a grand piano. I remember crying out (uncharacteristically),

"There's my castle!" overcome with emotion of recognition and surprise. Mrs. Daly responded matter-of-factly, "One day, I'll send it to you as a wedding gift." And she did. It was always *Mrs.—, Colonel—,* or *General—,* never first names. Naturally, *yes sirs, no ma'ams,* and never, *ever,* excuses.

Figure 14 Neuschwanstein Castle in Bavaria

When I behold the painting now, I imagine possibilities.

SUMMER

Haiku #10
Just in case (she says)
let me hold you in my arms.
Look! The sky is blue.

In the Northern Hills, April showers eventually show up in June. Hailstorms may damage seedlings and young apples. One year, the crop suffered a heavy hit, but the skins *mostly* healed over. Much of this fruit would be consigned to the apple press, or sold as *blems,* short for "blemished." Car windshields aren't as salvageable—a reason to keep vehicles garaged or in the shop when home—against the summer possibility. In winter, it's common sense.

Each year, I resolve to un-clutter shop, garage, and the house. I fail miserably. An ongoing chore for all seasons. Such would require a separate volume. Clutter *is* a concern, and one I am compelled to address as I grow older. The environmental axiom to leave no trace behind weighs on me. One day we shall certainly leave this place. Perforce, there are the collections, followed by *et cetera, et cetera, et cetera.* I do follow a *kind* of practice with regard to things, to mean: not strictly observed. For every item brought to the place, two must be given away, sold or tossed (if appropriate). Again, an ideal. Even adhered to fifty percent of the time, it proves helpful.

Keeping us close to home, summertime and fall are the busy seasons. We are obliged to water, though June can usually take care of itself thanks to more frequent rain showers. We can take a few days away after planting. If droughty, seeds must be watered, and if I've set out potted plants (of which I'm fond), they will later need daily dousing against the drying summer heat and hot breezes.

The studio/atrium houses several plants that may now be turned outdoors. The large olive tree, Olivia, can withstand the *Provençe*-like environment. She's a plant you admire more for structural beauty, and less for fruit. The tiny olives would require more effort than we are willing to make for the return. But beauty is beauty.

I hang laundry on the line once again for the sun-fresh fragrance. Pillows and comforters are aired, windows washed, the carpet steam-cleaned, the front and back porches swept, washed and stained, if necessary.

"Plants are also integral to reweaving the connection between land and people. A Place becomes a home when it sustains you, when it feeds you in body as well as spirit," writes Robin Wall Kimmerer in *Braiding Sweetgrass*. She is a member of the Citizen Potawatomi Nation, and a professor of Environmental Biology. When I contemplate her words, I sense deep kinship. Perhaps a kind of osmosis may begin after living, rooted, at last in one place. A wound of homesickness may be healed. Symbiosis may be the Earth's, and our, salvation.

Planting, weeding, thinning, hoeing, and mowing

- Jeff does most of the planting and weeding, but I experiment and plant part of the large garden a Native American way, i.e., The Three Sisters: Corn, Climbing Beans and Squash—the Buttercup winter variety. The three different seeds are planted together as companions; the beans grow up the corn stalk, while the squash shades the stems of each. Beans are nitrogen-fixing and act as fertilizer. As I say, it's an experiment. Jeff continues his practice of row planting, including, but not limited to, crookneck squash, zucchini, pumpkins, cantaloupe (whose long vines trail into the former garlic patch after its harvest), beets, tomatoes, eggplant, green peppers, beans, corn, peas, lettuce, basil, cilantro, and potatoes. The buried treasure of the latter elicits shrieks of joy and satisfaction.

- I tend my herbs and flowers, for the most part, until my husband loses patience with my procrastination at yanking grass from the well's posy bed and he digs in. If you do not wish to weed, alternatives exist; unfortunately, few are considered good practices. Using black tarp is detrimental to soil microbes, for instance. Herbicides are, well, herbicides. Planting perennials has proven a solution, whether herbs or flowers among the annuals (like zinnias and marigolds, favorites). The front yard flower garden could benefit from more space between plantings. I call it a "wild cottage garden," and leave it at that. If you must step into it, be careful to tap your stick in warning. A rattler will rattle— it is to be hoped. A neighbor tells me they're learning not to, as it could get them killed. *Wiseass snakes.*

- Thin lettuces, carrots, spinach, beets, et cetera. As superfluous edible young shoots break ground, pull, wash, and add them to your salads. Forage for other salad fixings: violet leaves and flowers; young lambs-quarter leaves; young dandelion and plantain leaves; dandelion and hollyhock flowers. Consult the numerous herbals and plant books for descriptions.

- As a last resort, Jeff occasionally elects to spray Sevin, an insecticide, on infestations of white aphids on the wild plums, or black aphids on the cherry trees and bushes, when chance of losing the plant is apparent. A useful remedy is garlic oil spray. (Handy, if you raise garlic; find it in the Remedies chapter.)

- Remove pests manually, such as potato beetles and the like. Black blister beetles attack the soapwort (Bouncing Bet) and Elderberries. Jeff sprays the Bets, but shakes the bugs off the Elderberries into a bag, and then stomps on the bag. This year, we had fewer bugs. It's a mystery. Blister beetles may be deterred by a spray containing Spinosad. This chemical breaks down within a couple of days. Full disclosure: we have not used this, but it is an alternative. *Do use gloves* if picking them off by hand.

- The tree cherries ripen near the end of June. After harvest, we "sit and pit" on the front porch, using our fingers to coax the pit from the flesh, having abandoned the fancy contraption designed to frustrate. Thank you to our Dutch friend, Katinka, for demonstrating the obvious. Wear aprons or old shirts against the inevitable squirting. Cherries are easily frozen in a single layer on a cookie sheet, then bagged and labeled. Jeff concocts a rich, dairy-free, frozen dessert with chocolate chips, cherries, corn syrup and almond drink in the ice cream machine. *Yum.*

- Root crops benefit from hoeing to loosen the adjacent soil, allowing for growth. When I've neglected to do this, erratic/erotic carrots result.

- The garlic is harvested near the Fourth of July, when at least two of the long, dagger-like leaves have turned brown and drooped. We plant two varieties in the fall: Roja and Asian Tempest. Reserve the largest bulbs each year to replant in the fall, for better yield.

The choice to continue planting garlic rests with the gardener, but we find it a willing crop for the area, not prone to summer hailstorms, early frosts or varmints. We bought the first seed stock almost thirty years ago. It's a favorite treat among friends and family, and sells well at farmer markets.

Spade in hand, Jeff follows the rows and gingerly digs down to loosen the soil, to more easily pull up the bulbs. These are sorted; the "hard neck" Asian Tempest goes into the wheelbarrow, to be hung to cure for two weeks in the garage, imparting a wonderful, if pungent fragrance to the space. A less good keeper, the variety must be consumed within three to four months. The soft neck *Roja* is good to braid and Jeff begins the task right away, sorting smaller bulbs from larger ones. He has mastered the technique, though afterward, his hands ache. The garlic bed is eventually tilled, and trailing melon and squash vines make their slow crawl over the soil. The garden's just-harvested side is also watered, if rain is lacking, to benefit the vines, certainly, but also for the health of soil microbes.

Roasted garlic is excellent spread on bread, and I like to make garlic honey to battle colds, sore throats and flu. Simply as an alternative to fruity jam, it is most worthwhile. It is antibacterial, antiviral, antiseptic, and soothing as a tea when a tablespoon is mixed with boiling water. Adding chopped ginger to the mix takes the flavor and healing properties to another realm altogether. It's a favorite remedy, with or without the ginger.

For a monthly fee, we have engaged a garbage disposal system, in lieu of the landfill pit and the chore of burning trash. The dumpster, visible at the highway turn-off, is an unattractive luxury. I've wondered if I could paint it with a *trompe d'oeil* scene, a camouflage of sorts, to fool the eye of passers-by. As stated earlier, we recycle much, but there is always Le Trash. We haul the garbage to the dumpster as needed and carry the compost bucket to its bin beside the large garden.

My present effort is to reduce our use of plastic containers and bags. We've saved enough empty milk jugs for the yearly cider needs and a cache of drinking water, but it's unconscionable and untenable how much plastic winds up in landfills and the oceans. My first goal is to replace all plastic jugs with glass jars.

A simple drinking straw lodges itself in a sea turtle's nostril. Plastic flossing pics finds their insidious way into the stomachs of sea birds. We can, and must, do better. It's a matter of the will.

OUR OWN PARADE

W̲e had been stationed in North Carolina for a year when our *nounou* Micheline arrived from France to live with us and . . . to have her baby. Just in time, by the swollen, maternal look of her as she carefully descended from the Piedmont Airlines prop plane in Raleigh, to make her ballooning way toward us ecstatic—if gawking—children.

Not once did I detect shame or judgment pointed toward our beloved *nounou,* given the times, else we were simply protected from it (more likely). I don't recall feeling one way or another about her unwed status. Micheline and *our* new baby Paola were what mattered to us. Funnily enough, much later my mother adopted Micheline's nickname, "Mimi," for herself—more *chic* than "Grandma."

This living arrangement coincided with my father's orders to Viet Nam in 1962, to serve as an advisor to the United States Joint Chiefs of Staff. Micheline's help proved invaluable to my mother, and Paola's birth and infancy added welcome distraction. (*Easy for me to say.*) The baby's father was French-Algerian. Micheline and he would eventually marry when she returned to France, but later divorce. Three children from a later marriage range close in age to Jeff's and mine, granting them a "cousin" distinction, with Micheline as "elder sister" to my siblings and me. Tragically, Paola passed away several years ago, far too young, of mesothelioma.

I count my father as one of the first American casualties of our nation's Viet Nam conflict, his third war—after WWII and Korea. The jolting of Army helicopters took its toll on his spine and he was evacuated, after six months, to San Antonio for surgery and recovery. In those days, post-op therapy meant being strapped to a circular bed, to be regularly turned like a roast on a spit. My mother made the trip to see him, once directing him, point blank, *"You son-of-a-bitch, you better not die and leave me with all these children!"* The epithet and demand were tongue-in-cheek, such was her humor, but it got his attention. He lived to survive three different bouts with cancer.

But something in him had died.

Decades later, following his death, I learned through reading his Viet Nam letters to my mother, how furious and heartsick he had become after uncovering graft and "funny business" during the few short months he'd served in Southeast Asia; to wit, that a company in Louisiana was exporting rice to Viet Nam at exorbitant cost (proverbial coals to Newcastle); that U.S. pork was being sold to Viet Nam, again, at obscene profit for the sellers. These are only two instances. *Beware the military industrial complex,* indeed, warned Dwight D. Eisenhower.

My father's indignation and reports were summarily ignored.

I believe he experienced a short-circuiting of his sensibilities, and it contributed to his great wound. *"What ails thee?"* Percival might have best asked his uncle, the Grail King; but disillusionment accompanied the existential pain, and Dad's response to the question was left unarticulated. At least to his children. He began to combine the (overly, in my view) prescribed pain killers with alcohol to numb recurrent back pain, constant headache from WWII shrapnel, and, his rage. It only fed the latter. The brilliant host of the program and app, *On Being,* Krista Tippett has observed that "anger is often what pain looks like when it shows itself in public."

While seldom speaking of Viet Nam, Dad would readily discuss his role in WWII and Korea. Viet Nam made no sense, apart from aiding the South Vietnamese against the Chinese Communists. Between his patriotism and intelligence, there yawned an abyss. "Intelligence" in both senses.

At an age when this undeclared war and its consequences were prompting cognitive dissonance in my own young sensibilities (being the daughter of a decorated colonel), I took refuge in school for the structure and peace it granted me. I largely ignored the protests and discussions at my high school, fearing condemnation, truth be told. Bomb threats—thankfully nothing more—were a near-weekly occurrence between 1968 and 1971, the year I graduated. However, before that milestone could happen, our family would be upended once more.

Is the migratory instinct cultivated in armed forces personnel? Maybe, just maybe, it's nigh impossible, psychologically, to stay put after being uprooted every three or four years—the average length of military assignment at the time—but I'm hitching the cart in front of the horse.

In 1964 Dad was granted 100% medical disability status from the Air Force during his last assignment to the air base in Georgia. My parents celebrated this classification, I recall, for the retirement benefits, despite the painful prerequisite to obtain it. At age forty-six, having served thirty years in the Air Force (he had joined at sixteen), he might survive many more years (it was to be hoped, and he did). Raising six children, however, required income above his pension.

Mom became the area *Atlanta Constitution* distributor, and brother André and I each delivered the early morning newspapers on our bicycles. I garnered strange looks, and suffered ridiculous comments, as "a female paper carrier." I mucked out horse stalls at a stable for a dollar an hour and babysat my guitar teacher's children up the street. *Never have I ever* needed to walk miles through deep snow to classes (well, yes, later, at the University of Wyoming), but I hauled my guitar in its heavy wooden case to and from grade school, nearly a mile and a half away, every Friday, where I played for St. Joseph's School guitar Mass. With my four sisters and brother in tow, we were our own parade.

SUMMER II

Apples set on apace now, often four or five to a stem. This is called "overbearing." (*I* may be overbearing at times, a completely different matter.) Thin to one or two fruits per stem for better size and less possibility of breakage; also, to lessen the chance of early fruit drop. Do it before the young fruit exceeds one inch in diameter. Leave the "king bloom" (the largest specimen) and allow six to eight inches between remaining fruit. This is the suggested practice and, I admit, an ideal. The "new" dwarf-cherry orchard, a nursery, celebrates its tenth birthday in 2021. The Romeo and Juliet varieties are crosses between sweet and sour cherries. *Tasty.*

- The single Summer Apple Tree (whom I call *Persephone*) bears in August and begins to drop her fruit with any tiny provocation. These are cooking apples and too mealy, for my taste, to eat out of hand. They make good applesauce, pies, and apple butter. Sautéed as fried slices, they can readily turn to mush if cooked too long.

- Knowing when to begin dragging round the hoses is a matter of observation and attention to the rain gauge. Normally, in early July. You might listen to the trees, as thirst is a universal language. I find having a routine works best for me and have divided the yard and orchard into six watering sectors. A personal preference, and someone might adopt a different tack. Some years bring heavier rainfall and I'm given a day off.

- Most of the grapes are fitted with drip irrigation, those on the lower vines below the large garden, and two vines skirting the hillside. The front yard Nanking cherries and chokecherries rely on drip irrigation as well. Jeff installed a watering system in both gardens, composed of plastic pipe and sprinklers, upon which the end is a hose connection. We may rely on rain in June and part of July, with intermittent watering. Below is my schedule for the orchard and yard plantings. Watering is best done in the evening, when moisture is better absorbed overnight, but anytime is better than not.

Mondays: Water first two rows of apple trees in the orchard (nearest the garage). Five minutes of full water force onto the area around the trunk. Take care not to gouge a hole too near the base of the trunk as, later, if the soil isn't properly in place, air, or a critter discovering a ready-made tunnel, might cause mischief. Stay within a reasonable watering circumference and use a timer. I like to take reading material, listen to a podcast, or just daydream. You could always weed around the trunks. The accepted practice is to dig out a circle that reaches the widest circumference of the leaves' drip line, and in this way, we water the roots instead of what's growing there. This said, I love the Sweet William flowers that grow under several trees. They attract fritillary butterflies that explode in an orange cloud when you walk by, like fairies all in a dither.

Tuesdays: Next two rows.

Wednesdays: The following row, plus trees along the north side of garden and west into the vineyard. The weather vane on the shop roof is adjusted to Four of the Seven Directions. (The Fifth, Sixth and Seventh are Above, Below and Within, in case you wonder.)

Thursdays: Hillside plantings: Omit the older, established vines, recognized by their maturing, two-three-inch "feet" or trunks. By a certain age, normal rainfall will suffice. (Normal is subjective, recall.) Also, water the younger vines; a drip irrigation plug-in found at the north fencing, in line with the northwest corner of the large garden. Make sure both valves are open (parallel to the hose), so the poplars along the fencing also get watered. Set a handy timer for two hours. I carry one with me.

Fridays: Back yard plantings.

Saturdays: The front yard. A row of chokecherries and Nanking cherries are watered by drip irrigation—the hose fittings are located beside the metal gate leading to the terrace and small cabin (my study).

We check weather reports daily, sometimes hourly, in summer for the forecast. Garden watering is separate from these more intentional chores. Jeff has made the garden task easier by installing hoses and sprinklers, as well as easy-on/off fittings. Poke a finger into the garden soil. If it's damp, you may postpone the chore; otherwise, twenty to thirty minutes for each section suffices. This only after the seeds have sprouted and are well established. However. a daily sprinkle on newly planted seeds and transplants will coax sprouting.

The propane tank lies buried beside the parking pad, adjacent the flower bed on the west side. We have it filled in summer, as the expense is less, but a thousand-gallon tank can be a large bill. Budgeting for it, taxes, insurance, travel, and gifts is recommended, *she says, airily.* The furnace/air conditioner and kitchen stove rely on propane, the rest on electricity—the reason for woodstoves. As of this writing, we have duly considered and installed solar photovoltaic panels. Meanwhile, we work at using as little energy as required and, not to sound alarmist, we would do well to consume far less of everything. I consider it all ephemeral; *it* being the whole experiment/experience of life, but there remains the burning, moral question of descendants, and my shaky soapbox teeters beneath me. We require *some* form of electricity to pump water from our 115-foot deep well—an overriding concern. (Watch this space for further developments; my writing is organic.)

While I prefer a wilder, more primitive lawn, allowing the native grasses to grow tall in the orchard and yards, Jeff objects. The possibility—and probability—of snakes, the venomous kind, calls for the wiser objective of visibility. We've never tried the old (*Indian?*) trick of encircling the space with a hose or rope (snakes will avoid their crossing, it is purported); besides, we'd need a lot of rope, though we do haul around yards and yards of hose when watering. *Hmmm.*

We douse the lawns with less intention, though adequately, and mow less frequently toward September. For the sake of tidiness, we will mow in autumn once. (Or not.) Gold leaves from cottonwood, ash, and black locust cover the grass, to disappear by spring, gone with the Wyoming wind. I love the painterly, Seurat-like stippling dotting the ground. But I get ahead of myself, season-wise.

Several plants and trees benefit from regular fertilizing. Fall and spring is traditional, if the ideal. Jeff's use of the pruned limb mulch around the base of the orchard trees fulfills this purpose. I like to use Miracle Grow on certain plants, namely, the three Burning Bush shrubs, and rose food on roses, bulb food on bulbs. Community Flower Gardener Extraordinaire, Walt Daknis, mixes a recipe for fertilizer that is effective; but heed my warning: *Do not let it get wet, for it smells of death,* ~~lightly~~ warmed-over, and the scent molecules inhabit your nostrils for weeks. The instructions follow in REMEDIES. The storeroom on the back porch holds all manner of gardening supplies, including the fertilizers, hand tools, and the like. Onward:

- Replace blades on the lawn mower and sharpen the chain saw. Gardening tools (hoes, spades) perform better when sharpened and cleaned of caked-on mud. (I've tried both ways and know this to be true.)

Summer invites visitors and houseguests. A childhood friend of Jeff's hails the place, "The Tuscany of Wyoming!" High praise, indeed. I've visited Tuscany. Here, we lack the cypress trees and, oh—that area's ancient and present culture. I *have* likened the environs to Scotland or Wales, never having been, and was summarily corrected; "Too many trees," quipped Andy, who might have known, having recently returned from Scotland. *"Clearly, he didn't visit the Caledonian Forest!"* observed a friend.

Gazing out over what early Black Hills explorers and geologists back in 1874 called *natural parks*, meadowlands punctuated by groves of trees, I draw my own comparisons, perhaps as a waking daydream, perhaps as means to teleport—at least in my mind—to some distant land. *But this* is *Wyoming,* I am reminded. And not so gently, during the throes of a violent summer thunderstorm or raging winter blizzard. The weather—if you'll forgive the fallacy—is a most formidable character, not to be mocked, ignored, or summarily dismissed.

As an early-warning system against tornadoes, and more likely, a probable hail storm (often accompanying twisters), an emergency radio—a useful membership gift from Wyoming Public Radio—has proven such on several occasions. If you have time, cover the garden plants with a tarp. We store a collection of drop cloths, tarps, and old tablecloths for the purpose. Yet nothing will prepare you for the sight of shredded greenery and battered squash vines.

Earth, Wind, Fire, Water

On the Fourth of July, firework displays light up the sky at nearby Devils Tower National Monument. The booms reverberate around the rock, *I* believe on account of its geology, phonolite porphyry. The stone "rings" upon being struck, but logic, or fancy suggests its mere gigantic presence would unsettle the physics of the place, if confronted with a constant bombardment of gunpowder. In any case, it makes for quite the sound and light spectacle.

The area is tightly packed with tourists and locals, all vying for the best viewing. We attend most years but can sometime hear the explosions from our front porch, ten miles away as the crow flies. The sound travel may have to do with humidity or lack thereof. (I could run an experiment.) Some years the event is cancelled for droughty conditions and risk of fire, always a concern when living among trees, 400 million-plus, by estimate in a 1999 study. Forested lands in the Hills cover 1.16

million acres. However, a recent assessment (2022) found fewer cubic feet of timber available to harvest over the last twenty years—and into the present—due to both pine beetle degradation, and forest fires

Picturesque Cook Lake is located an hour away in the Bear Lodge Mountains of Wyoming's Black Hills National Forest. Our favorite nearby "water feature," it was closed for several years due to a landslide, or "land failure," as it's called here. A saturated hillside above one bank of the lake slid into the large pond, buckling the land, as it were, to leave a gouged-out, raw cut in the woods above, exposing twisting and torn roots. Ponderosa, aspen, birch, ash, and oak jut akimbo from the disturbed soil, to continue their lives however they may. I think on the sad parallel of children's lives upended and their having to endure broken futures on inhospitable soil.

The Forest Service keeps tabs on shifting land, and this last year deemed the lake safe for day use by reopening a campground away from the landslide area.

We often camped at the lake when the children were young. Friends joined us, or we joined them, for the all-important exercise of getting away from it all, in order to return home with renewed appreciation for running water and indoor toilets (a corrective benefit of visiting the Casper Mountain cabin as well). Cook Lake is fed by Beaver Creek and dammed, creating the reservoir. It is stocked with trout, catfish, and sunfish. Shad too, I hear.

One summer we took our grandson for an evening picnic and to fish. Parker is a great enthusiast of adventure and full of joy, with a subtle sense of humor. We look forward to taking his younger sisters, Austin and Haven. Their parents may come if they like. . . .

Figure 15 At Cook Lake

FURTHER AFIELD

Disregarding the novelist Thomas Wolfe, my father decided to go home again. In the fall of 1968 I'd attended, as a freshman, my oh-so-pined-for first public school for a mere three months when Dad informed us children at dinner that we were moving to Louisiana, where he'd accepted a job. To be fair, he asked our opinions as though we had some agency in his decision. We may have been shocked, but we deferred to his wishes. Of course. He departed before us, to leave Mom to make necessary arrangements.

Several weeks after he was settled, Mom received a phone call from an aunt in Louisiana, where Mama Ease and other family members lived. "Paul's been in a serious accident, Millie. You better come on."

Following a whirlwind of activity and accompanying dread, Mom managed to collect what she thought we'd need for the near future and hired someone to "pack up the house." Military wives are old hands at this and, if not talented, then resigned to it. You simply soldier on. Her expression was, once again, pained and rife with worry.

We finally pulled out of our driveway on a dark, early December evening. A boarder, with whom I was having a messed-up relationship for my age, jogged beside the vehicle until Mom accelerated, heading south. (More on this below.)

We drove past the Atlanta stadium to sounds of cheering. My high school team was busy vying for the state football championship. I could refer to my yearbook, but I honestly cannot remember if we won or not. I think we did. The phrase, "second to none," confounded me for many years.

In Louisiana at the time, you could obtain a driver's license at fifteen, and so I did, to help chauffeur my younger brother and sisters. My father taught me to drive with his usual studied patience and regard reserved for flight students. My poignant memory: just us, our Oldsmobile station wagon, and a two-lane road all the way to Monroe and back. I believe the psychology of teacher to pupil provided Dad a smoother avenue on which to negotiate our purpose that day. Like a cloudless sky, free of obstacles.

Mom *loved* Emmy Lou Harris' rendition of "Leaving Louisiana in the Broad Daylight." After nine months of fish-out-of-water living, or maybe, "in the water," given the debilitating Gulf states' humidity, we high-tailed it back to Georgia. The job had been ill-represented, admitted Dad, and he resigned. While in Lake Charles, Mom had returned to nursing, preferring the quieter night shift.

In late August, before the school year began, the dark smell of boxwoods and our Georgia home's fuggy mustiness greeted us, and oh, we had missed it. "Old" gets in your blood, with regard to houses, furniture, and particular ideals. It was the proverbial zoo, readying six of us for school, and I suppose we managed. Mom had shown the presence of mind (or perhaps the presentiment) to hold our old house off the market. Not *that* old, it had been built in 1929 (the year of her birth) by the McNeal family, proprietors of a marble quarry in North Georgia. The front porch and bathroom floors were therefore splendid. Though we had no furniture, save beds and a table and chairs, we made do for months while the broken contract in Louisiana was being negotiated and decided. The newer house in Louisiana had never felt like home.

At last, all arrived, including the gorgeous antiques my parents had shipped from France in 1961, and we got on with it—life as a family—amid the growing storm of my father's illnesses and irrational behavior. At this time, he was also diagnosed with cancer, eventually beating three different bouts, as I've mentioned, but there emerged two persons: one, the sweetest, kindest man on Earth, and the other, a hurting, wounded soul who lashed out. He found work selling trucks and campers, and was good at it because he was good with people—if on occasion less patient with his own family—as is often the case.

In Daniel J. Levitin's bestselling *Successful Aging,* the author as neuroscientist sheds light on our brain's wonders, and, its responses to frailties. In the chapter on pain, he describes YLDs, or, years living with (or lost to) living with disability, what Levitin calls *disease span.* We read to enlighten ourselves and to improve our minds. I already knew my father couldn't help himself. Now I apprehend a bit more the reasons.

Likely the result of her nursing vocation, Mom exuded profound patience (if not a saintly equanimity), and she was able to find a separate peace, working the night shift at the nearby hospital. In delivering babies, she regained some joy and, I daresay, her sense of self.

After school, I clerked at a department store and, on spring and summer weekends, showed a Palomino Tennessee Walking horse stud. I practiced my guitar chords and fingerstyle picking, and I sang. Folk music brought me pleasure and solace. It still does.

Dinner time was often a genial gathering of eight around the kitchen table, with my youngest sister Nancy providing comic relief much of the time, our Balm of Gilead and gift of perspective. If I recall laughter and humor in one ear, I also hear their opposites in the other. Ours was a passionate household. (Read: noisy.) Our cousin, a university student in Atlanta, took the spare basement room, now vacant. Through the years, my parents offered the room to several students. Equipped with an outside entrance, the boarders came and went as they pleased.

The very first (whom I'll call Carl) sought other lodgings after we left for Louisiana. Upon our return, I continued to see him until I was sixteen. This relationship was as underground as a conscious acknowledgement of our father's illness. Carl was seven years older than I. For three years, from 1966 to 1969, I lived with the secret and told no one. Today I recognize it for what it was; more to do with power *over* and less with care.

After I learned he'd gotten married, this aforementioned "messed up relationship" drove me to an amateur suicide attempt, yes, even after I thought I'd broken free of him. There simply was no time for histrionics or the high school girl's propensity for drama (and one I rarely indulged). It was likely a "*cri de coeur*" to my parents that spurred my swallowing a half-bottle of aspirin.

That my psychology was never properly evaluated afterward and the incident summarily ignored, might give some pause, but the capacity in our family was simply not available. That Carl and I appeared to be merely "good friends" had been the acceptable version. The one time I was questioned about it, I lied to my mother. In mortification, I believe it was the only time I was ever blatantly untruthful to her. *To save her the pain? To protect her?* She had enough on her hands.

Not to gloss, slide, or skate over the rug, under which my experience and its brick wall had been swept, in my late twenties I finally sought therapy, as coping mechanisms and those maladaptive behaviors were interfering with sanity. Through the years, and five therapists later, I've achieved a certain peace around it all. Eschewing pharmaceutical anti-depressants, I prefer exercise and St. John's Wort, a common remedy in Germany against low-grade depression. Both remedies continue to be my allies. And yes, meditation.

How sensibilities will smooth and calm, like ever-slowing rings of water, long after the stone is flung, capriciously or not. You could imagine, as a young girl might, the sting and burning weight of a meteor as it plunges into an ocean, and the devastating, concentric waves such an event must produce and account for. To extend the metaphor (behind which I cower), I nearly drowned in the troughs and crests of these invisible (to others) waves for several years, long after the "cataclysm" of my sad story had ended, by my own force of will. Classmates, two in particular, tossed me life preservers. For their kindness and comfort, I am indebted to them.

The Scots have a saying: *Forgive your enemy, but remember the bastard's name.* I forgave the man decades ago, for my own soul. But I tell the tale in the interest of bearing fair witness to that too-young girl. She has watched me struggle before coming to forgive myself. It's an ongoing practice, isn't it?

My maternal grandparents, MoMo and Pawpaw, lived in Charleston, South Carolina. Pawpaw Jack succumbed to

Huntington's disease and was eventually hospitalized in Columbia, South Carolina. This weighed heavily on Mom; she adored her father. Once, she told me a story of her own first singing performance when she was thirteen, at their First Baptist Church. Pawpaw and MoMo were seated in a front pew waiting for their daughter to begin. Mom became nervous and Pawpaw smiled to reassure her. She took a deep breath, exhaled and declared, "I'll start as soon as that man there quits laughing at me," pointing to her father. He may have been grinning, but certainly not laughing. The congregation broke up, quieted and she was able to begin.

She went on to sing for radio spots.

My mother coached (and coaxed) my first "public" performance. I was six and attending the French school in Moret-sur-Loing. For the *programme de Noël,* I learned to sing "Deck the Halls," in English. Duly petrified, I recall standing, rubber-legged, before seated parents and teachers. Alone. No accompaniment. However, Momma sat beaming at me. Encouragement is everything.

When I was seventeen, I lived in Paris for several weeks with an older French couple of my parents' acquaintance. Heretofore, I had timidly embraced and sought refuge in a less rebellious worldview. That summer I revised my personal philosophy. Monsieur and Madame Flamant were adamant I not befriend any of the university students who had brought Paris to its knees two short years before (regarding teaching standards and expectations, leading to a cultural paradigm shift), but I saw little evidence of protests or strikes, France having resumed her oh-so practical workings. I would lug my guitar in its heavy case onto the Metro and choose a park among the myriad opportunities.

On one such day, a police woman told me it was illegal to busk there; I assured her I was not (playing for tips), and she politely asked me then to close my guitar case, to make it seem less evident. I did. She smiled. No problem.

On another excursion requiring the subway (the apartment was located on the western edge of Paris), I had just arrived down at the Metro platform to take a train to some destination I don't recall, when the doors opened and out stepped a couple of classmates from my home town in Georgia, one of whom had moved to Alabama with his family two years before. *"Renée??!"* asked my astonished friend. A second classmate of mine stood beside him. A more unlikely surprise I could not have imagined and I definitely wouldn't write it in a novel. Maybe. It bespeaks, "Of all the gin joints," et cetera. My friends were on a student tour, ergo, on a schedule, so we couldn't spend much time analyzing the phenomenon. I had the rest of my life for that.

One of them and I were elected Valentine King and Queen in eighth grade, and the other I had supported in geometry class. Both friends were the sort you're loath to keep something from, as I had done. By then I had extricated myself (or so I believed) from the clandestine relationship and was cautiously dating someone my own age. At this same time, my new beau was traveling and studying French with yet another student group in the south of France. He and I finagled to meet for two days in Archachon, requiring I take the train. We also met for two days in Paris.

Of course, it was magical, in case you wonder. Full of the satisfaction of longing. *Oh, to be young and in love in Paris. . . .*

The occasions I visited Micheline and her daughter Paola in Fontainebleau rang nostalgic with bursts of laughter and acceptance of what I was, a naïve seventeen-year-old. She still lived in the small apartment where her Italian mother had raised nine children. Paola's father lived nearby. I spent a weekend once, and Micheline and I went to a discothèque in Fontainebleau. Located underground, it took up the entire cellar of a two-, or three-hundred-year-old structure.

I've often contemplated how architecture colors and informs our awareness of the human condition, but not that night, among strobes and colored lights, too-loud music and close bodies. I remember the thick haze and smell of cigarette smoke and body odor. Our daughter danced at the same one twenty-five years later, in 1995, with Micheline's teenaged children.

I gained weight that summer of '70 (*oh, that bread! the cheese! my homesickness!),* my travel diary recounting the frequent occasions for sampling French cuisine. And wine. With respect, may I impart an important lesson that (some) young French students learn at home: initially, water is mixed with wine, the amount of water gradually reduced. They learn at home what it feels like, and how to read their level of intoxication. Madame Flamant taught me how to *sip* brandy as well. "You take just a *very little* on the tip of your tongue," she instructed me in French, "and allow it to spread to the back of your tongue, and then, you swallow."

She and Monsieur Flamant concocted their own orange brandy, preserving orange peels over a kitchen curtain rod, to later infuse in alcohol. I never learned which they preferred to use—brandy? or vodka?

We shared a name, Renée Flamant and I. Monsieur Flamant was Michel, but I was expected to call them *Monsieur* and *Madame*. The degrees of formality in French society are best not ignored. *Comme il faut* is still the rule. Loosely, it means "properly."

Madame Flamant had little to no English. Michel spoke well, but my ostensible purpose that summer was to study French. I would have benefited from a more structured curriculum and environment in that regard. I *craved* to hear English, and would sit, or stand, half a day on the Metro just to visit the American Embassy where they provided a rack of English paperbacks. Being shy, even after I'd had the occasional tongue-loosening glass of wine, my hosts' heroic efforts to have me socialize were met with questioning faces as to my intelligence (or lack thereof). I certainly didn't return home resembling, or sounding like, Audrey Hepburn's *Sabrina,* svelte and chic—*àu contraire*—but I was strangely calm and sanguine, even ambivalent (my usual *modus operandi)* when the classmate I'd been seeing ended our relationship in the fall.

The weight dropped with little effort once I returned to the rigors of academia, extracurricular activities, and home fires, and I blithely resumed a more heightened concentration on studies, music, art, and taking photographs for the yearbook. I had sorely missed my family, but not the dramas. Unfortunately, weight fluctuations have persisted for over fifty years, contributing to heart and soul troubles. The thorn in my side.

I am indebted to many teachers, as we all must be, but especially to my senior year English teacher for initiating her honors class students into the world of

Joseph Campbell and transpersonal psychology. She had us read, and thoroughly ingest, his *Hero with a Thousand Faces*. Archetypal mythology, and our own hero's journey through the drama of life, expanded my worldview. From there, I inhaled Carl Jung's autobiography, *Memories, Dreams, Reflections*, while suffering the collective jaundiced eye of parents and friends.

At my high school Homecoming Assembly that October, after performing the event's theme, "Sounds of Silence" by Simon and Garfunkel, I received a standing ovation. Lacking the grace and presence of mind to bow and accept the applause, I instead scurried behind the curtains, flustered. Accepting praise is difficult. A simple Thank You is all that is necessary or expected. A classmate accused me of false modesty. I didn't know what he was talking about.

Why do some of us feel so unworthy? I would spend decades pondering the question. If not exactly a waste of time, then certainly counterproductive. Learning about distorted thinking patterns—and recognizing them—has helped me. I am an advocate of Cognitive Behavior Therapy as well as Jungian psychology, and Positive Psychology.

In 2007 I attended a week-long herbal workshop; "an intensive," in Woodstock, New York. Germane to my earlier discussion, I had an epiphany while there (what the apprenticeship was designed to provoke). Camping among several women, all strangers, during a laser-focused interval of time and purpose, can, and did, shake up prior self-awareness, or sadly—lack thereof. Here is what happened:

I had offered to make these meditative sounds I had learned, but I shortened my presentation, believing it might be tedious, dull or somehow unimportant.

Stopping, I said something to that effect. One of the women spoke afterward, softly.

"Don't *do* that—dismiss yourself like that." The others agreed.

I took it to mean not to demean or dismiss my agency (not the word she used, but apt). On my air mattress that night, I was reminded of how often I halt before completing a train of thought in conversation, to jump to another; or, of shortening a song I am singing for fear of needlessly "asserting" myself, of showing off, of being a bore. Humility and shame had become entangled and conflated. I was, in essence, afraid to take up space.

A Benedictine nun once told me, that by women, humility must be practiced differently than by men. A humble woman knows well what she is *incapable* of doing but, more important, humility demands she be conscious and aware of what she *can* do. Difficult and brave is the (humble) task of shining your light on it and yourself, then, to proceed with confidence. I don't mean to restrict this awareness to women; men are often just as susceptible, but I wonder if Jesus was referring to a woman when speaking of hiding one's light under a bushel basket?

So, humble. From human. From humus—*the Earth.* Grounded. I would live grounded. Rooted. And take my proper place.

AUTUMN

Indian summer denotes the passage of time between first frost and second, or third, snow. Traditional first frost arrives September 15. Milder than the first *hard* frost, but you pretty much know you are headed for winter. In the more than three decades we've lived here, October and November have mostly remained fall-*ish,* but they have also brought mighty blizzards. There are no surefire predictions. Our son the pilot likes the app, AccuWeather. So, there's that.

A few years ago, between Jeff's back surgery and his long recovery, I harvested the orchard, thanks to hired help from Joe and Kody. A first frost lowered temperatures to thirty-one degrees for two nights in a row. Frosty cold sweetens apples, converting their starch to sugar (in the winter varieties), insuring their characteristic crunch. We distribute signs in town and place an ad in local papers. Jeff fashioned a hinged sandwich board years ago to advertise near the mailbox at the highway: *Apples 4 Sale*→ on both sides. Pithy.

Instruction follows regarding the picking of apples. *Thou shalt not simply yank them from the tree.* And never shake a limb to dislodge the fruit. Just. Don't. The tree may be injured and will give less the following year, or not at all. Now, pretend you are staring up (most of the time it's "up," and not easy, low-hanging fruit). Look for the short sub-branch between apple and limb, a woody piece about three-quarters of an inch long. This is the spur. If this comes off, you endanger future production. What you want to do is twist the apple and take the stem *from* the spur. Simple. But requiring a certain mindfulness. We own one of those long, caged apple pickers, but reserve it for only a few in the tops of the trees. The less used, the better.

Use your palm to cradle the fruit, and not merely your fingers. The pressure can bruise the apple. If you meet resistance, allow the apple to ripen longer. Apples will not ripen after they are picked, at least naturally. You could always taste one if you question their readiness. Again, they ripen at slightly different speeds, so it's a judgment call, depending on the forecast.

Take care how you unload your picked apples. If you drop them into a basket, they'll bruise. A solution is to set a low table or chair at a height to easily catch the fruit.

Apart from the beans that the rabbits raided this year (a first), the garden yield didn't disappoint. The garage refrigerator holds pots of tomatoes, green beans, and cucumbers until they can be dealt with. The sharp scent of a tomato leaf after it's been nudged is one of the freshest surprises I know. Discovering and picking the rose-colored and purple heirlooms is akin to an Easter-egg hunt. Again, carefully twist the fruit off the plant, or better, use a knife. Less chance of tearing the plant.

I'm here to tell you it takes one hour to preserve seven quarts of tomatoes in a pressure canner, from slipping the skins in a quick boiling water dip, to turning off the fire under the canner (at twelve pounds of pressure for ten minutes at our altitude—4,000 feet). It becomes second nature after a few decades, though canning may be daunting at first.

Loosen the soil first around carrots and other root crops by gently spading on one or two sides. It helps if the soil is slightly damp; at least not bone-dry. Beans may be plucked by hand; the younger, the more tender, but in my experience, a few overly long usually wind up in the basket. And everyone has heard of the giant zucchinis that find their way onto the porches of neighbors. This is not an urban, or even a rural, legend. These I grate and freeze to use in zucchini bread.

Between harvesting and putting up corn, beans (normally, a bushel or more), tomatoes, potatoes, and beets, among other vegetables), my writing and Jeff's seemingly Sisyphean tasks (when he's not laid up), "the days are just packed," to quote one of my favorite comic strips, *Calvin and Hobbes*. I reserve mornings to work in my study, located a hundred feet from the house, originally meant for visiting family or guests. A twin bed serves when needed, but I claim the sweet space.

Our hardworking Yankee neighbor who passed away too soon, Ben Hummel built several of the ten-by-sixteen-foot cabins. By a civil engineering feat of determined know-how, he hauled the shell over to us one fine day, nestling it among ponderosas and bur oaks on a pitch of land—a terrace—overlooking the "burn," a mostly dry ravine. With the help of carpenter, luthier, and friend, Tom Cowell (who installed the larger-than-strictly-necessary stovepipe I threatened to paint purple), Jeff insulated and framed in the rough-cut walls and ceiling. They added a wrap-around deck and extended the roof to protect the latch-string door, thus providing a proper "front stoop." In summer and fall, a shade-sail lessens sun glare onto my desk and computer.

Virginia Woolf was correct and perceptive: women do need "a room of one's own." Men as well, apparently. Witness the rise of Man Caves and She Sheds, as though only current popular culture discovered these boosts to one's mental health. Everyone benefits from a margin of peaceful solitude to encourage and engage creativity, or merely to daydream. That the notion has become a luxury underscores my deep gratitude. My mother used to escape to her small bathroom, lock the door and *just sit* on the close-lidded toilet a few moments (I questioned her once), before resuming the work of running an eight-member household, including a revolving door of dogs, cats, and boarders. I know of one author who wakes during the night to write from midnight to four a.m., like a faithful monk praying *matins*. Time and place trade places.

When learning a new song, or working up an old one, I prefer solitude, or privacy, if you will. At college, I'd retreat to the dorm's stair well. The acoustics were fun, besides. Music students are assigned practice rooms; art students, studios. *Io studio* translates, "I study," in Italian. The *certainty* of mistakes is offset by privacy, where learning, perfecting, and polishing might bloom. An obvious analogy, but consider the fact: roots prefer dark soil in order to grow. (Hydroponics aside.)

Solitude and loneliness, of course, are different. One may arise from the other. An existential dread of a looming Great Lonesome goaded me to finally seek and find solace in writing, not only through daily journaling efforts (since 1989), but toward a more expansive challenge—the novel. My tired old joke suggests the house contains far too many chairs for a reason. For my characters. Never mind the obvious solution—that I might simply host vast dinner parties.

Loneliness, writes Senator Ben Sasse in *Them*—his valiant effort to heal the divide in our country at present—is what happens when someone suffers a lack of meaning in their lives. I would add *purpose*. The two are related. *Not me! I'm much too fulfilled!* cries my extrovert side. As means to counter an utter denial of empty-nest syndrome, paired with a gnawing desire to write, I began. But only after sitting out the whole of 2014, absorbed in reading. Also, in watching all four seasons of *Battlestar Galactica*. Long live Starbuck!

Jeff thought I'd checked out on him and, to be fair, I had. All but the most essential obligations were summarily ignored. I read four complete series, occasionally staying up until five in the morning to finish one of the books. "Magnificent obsession" or not, I read for instruction, for inspiration and yes, I hear, *escape?* from some, but the temporary madness served a purpose. I owe a debt of gratitude to Diana Gabaldon, author of the *Outlander* series, for liberally sharing her unorthodox methods à propos her process. I learned much; for instance, I discovered I prefer to write *organically*.

My husband the biologist winces at my appropriation of the word. *Roots* grow organically, any ole which way. We, who permit inspired literary snippets and passages to eventually find each other, write organically. In other words, we don't know where our words will take us much of the time. I revel in the mystery and anticipation of it all. I rejoice in well-turned phrases (when the rare one appears), and I delight in mythical solutions. A hero's journey, indeed.

In January of 2015, I set out on my quest. Whereas our decision to purchase this property and raise our children was fundamentally an outward journey, the writing remains an inward, mostly mental voyage. I began work on a story. Over six years, it has grown to three novels of my Riven Country series.

For Christmas that first year, Jeff presented me with a small propane heater. We could attach the tank outside the cabin, to change out when needed. "If I'd known that was all it'd take," he laughed, with a degree of surprise at my discipline. It hadn't occurred to me either, believing wood fire my only option. Shutting myself away from nine 'til noon, every day but weekends, I contentedly forged a new habit and the magical gift of *flow* lent me its grace, the "optimal state of consciousness," coined by psychologist Mihály Csíkszentmihályi. I occasionally edit at the house, where I can also use the Internet when required.

A fairy, or angel—literary or not—had whispered in my ear for years, if not decades, and in truth, I *had* once tried to write in the tiny cabin. In winter (when temperatures can fall below zero), the fire in the cabin's wood stove takes a couple hours to warm the room. By then, I would be spent, creatively, and frustrated by my efforts, however mindful of masterpieces penned by freezing fingers. Probably in Russia. Long novels— driven by the very cold they often describe.

There is always the tedious part to any worthy endeavor, and writing is no different. For example, I've learned that morning circumstances color my headspace—regarding concentration and available inspiration. It's a *writerly* thing, I propose, then realize I'm mistaken. My pilot son, his safety-expert wife, my daughter and her husband, each in law enforcement, require (absolutely) the same deference: focused working sensibilities. "Nope, it's everyone," I conclude. Mindfulness can so easily dissipate, like steam, into thin air.

Conduits (think culverts, pipes, arteries, veins, et cetera) allow for better flow when not obstructed. I can hope it's a question of practice and that, eventually, I'll be able to write anywhere, under any circumstances, and ignore distraction. For now, the study is a gift I give to myself. In every season. An added value lies in returning home to Jeff and my obligations, renewed in spirit and satisfaction, with a sense of purpose and perspective. So, to return to this season. . . .

Fall Chores

• Clean stovepipes and gutters. First, be sure the wood stove door is closed and latched, or black soot will cover every square inch and prove a valid reason to curse. Choose a day when footing on the roof is dry, free from ice and snow; position the ladder against the lower, north-side garage gutter and haul up the chimney brush—a stiff, round one attached to a rope—for the purpose of dangling down the pipe. Pine burns stickily, coating the pipe with resin that can ignite if too much builds up. We also burn oak, which burns hotter, aiding in scouring the pipe, but not completely.

• Leaves from the few deciduous trees in the yard find their windblown way into the house gutters. 'Nough said. Except to exercise caution on the ladder.

• Normally, we don't rake leaves; I prefer to see them. A purely personal preference.

• Check the light bulb in the well pit behind the house. The blue steel cover is heavy; you may need help in lifting and moving it over.

• Plug in the heat tape on the back porch. This prevents freeze-ups in the water softener pipe, leading from the storeroom, underground, into the ravine, east of the house.

Later in the year, you'll take a hammer to the icy stalagmites forming below the spout.

Years ago, Jeff installed a sub-pump in the well, in case of (another) problem with the water. Once, upon returning from a trip, he discovered the underground well housing completely filled with water. After cutting off the electricity, he and son John bailed it out, using buckets. It took a long time. You don't want this to happen. When checking, if the light bulb in the housing is on, it's a safe bet the sub-pump is good to go. It's a good idea to leave a light burning during the winter, as it provides some heat against freezing. Take an extra bulb. Our daughter and I were conveniently away in France during this fiasco. *C'est la vie.*

Draining outside hose bibs is necessary against freeze-ups. (Please excuse my overstating the obvious when I do.) Frozen pipes on a remote homestead give the Devil joy. It requires ditch-digging, patience, multiple trips to hardware stores—some at a distance, at least one blessedly nearby, and more patience and money.

Jeff demonstrated the draining procedure to me one day and I suspect a diagram might serve better than written instruction; however, the pipe in question is labeled in the storeroom on the back porch (where it runs from the well). It's a matter of scurrying to and from the house faucets, and turning them on and off as the water fizzles to an end. Here are the steps:

1. In the storeroom, open the valve nearest the hot water heater.

2. Go open the faucet beside the front porch steps.

3. Back in the storeroom, open the second valve/faucet, close to the water heater, under the pipe.

4. Open the faucet in the studio/atrium (at ground-level, to the left of the door into the den). After draining (use a pan—there will be a little water), close the outdoor faucets "a bit."

We lift each hose, a few feet at a time, to allow water to drain, roll it up to store behind the house in the covered garden storage area, where we also keep a supply of pinecones. (As fire starter, these are handy, and handy is their source—the noble stand of ponderosas behind the house. Gathering them is a great activity for grandchildren and antsy adults.)

To repeat, we fertilize in fall to encourage a plant's journey into winter. By contrast, we *amend* soil, by adding nutrients, such as peat moss and/or green manures. Use Walt's concoction, or your preference. The tall Colorado blue spruce in the front yard (named *Christmas!)* and the two neighboring Thujas (commonly known as Arborvitaes) like deep-watering and Miracid. They stand in memory of our parents: John and Sammy Carrier, and Paul and Millie Latiolais.

Trees may be planted in the fall, if necessary. Because of our harsher climate, we normally plant in the spring, to give roots ample time to establish. Here is our method:

One does not simply dig a hole, stick in said sapling and fill with dirt. But yes, first dig a hole, deeper than you might think necessary. Two feet deep will suit most purposes, and this depends on the size of your sapling, of course. Ours have ranged from an eight-inch Arbor Day seedling (which has grown into an over forty-foot Colorado Blue spruce), to five or six-foot specimens.

Jeff hauls a wheel barrow of good garden soil to our well-considered site: prevailing winds may contribute to "cold pockets," an area where dense frigid air is trapped, spelling too adverse a climate for susceptible species. A tree might prefer the protection of a building, but you can look for "hardy," when choosing your varieties. Mind the planting/hardiness zone! Ours is 4; 9, 10, and 11 are found much further south. Elevation is a concern as well. (At 4,000 feet, as noted earlier, our chances are better than the rest of the state. Excluding the mountains, Wyoming's average elevation stands at 6,700 feet—not conducive to widespread gardening ventures—but being humans, we will try.) Take particular care where pipes, gas lines, or telephone cables may be buried (roots can wreak havoc with septic systems, for instance).

We lay down a small tarp to hold the diggings, making it easier to take away. Next, fill much of the hole with water and allow it to soak in. After replacing two-thirds of the dirt with garden soil, mound it pyramid-like. Jeff gently spreads the fragile roots over this. (Do place the seedling or sapling roots in a bucket of water when the tree arrives. Yes, some come from nurseries as "bare root," rather than potted. I refer to these for this discussion. In either case, water both examples right away.)

It helps if I hold the sapling in place as Jeff gingerly shovels the soil back in.

When the tree (or shrub—same directions) is well entrenched and standing upright and spry, with the knobby graft above ground (nurseries will usually mark this with tape), continue filling in with garden soil, intermittently adding more water and mixing the mud with your hands, to release any air pockets that might have formed. We leave a two or three-inch deep well, usually twenty-four inches in diameter, for water to collect in, again, depending on the size of the sapling. And, depending on the weather, moisture-wise, new trees benefit from daily watering through the season.

The last step is to trim taller saplings back to three or four branches. (Consult a proper reference for a schematic.) This allows them to put more energy into the limbs you are trying to develop. Recall, if you snip the leading branch, the side limbs will eventually overtake it. It depends on the shape of tree you wish to grow. Never snip the terminal bud of a conifer, unless you want it to spread all over the place, as if it's totally confused.

"The best time to plant a tree is twenty years ago," goes the proverb. Probably Chinese. "The second best is now," follows. Often interpreted as a nudge, to free someone from the paralysis of remorse or indecision, I take care not to interpret it too literally, but how can I not? We planted all of the non-indigenous plants and trees around our yard and home in the first decades of our stewardship, with subsequent plantings to replace diseased trees, or to fill out the orchard. Jeff recently planted three young Bolleanas poplars, gifts from a long-time friend. *Thank you, John Curless.*

Speaking of disease, I've mentioned fire blight, a bacterial infection, against which we spray an antibiotic every spring. Unfortunately, our climate—hail, strong winds, and heavy rain—contributes to its ravages. Cedar-apple rust is a concern as well. Caused by a fungus, it leads to leaf drop and poor-quality fruits. Western red cedars (junipers) are prolific in the area and, if our orchard is susceptible, which in all likelihood is the case, we have learned to live with it. Since we can't remove all cedars in a three-mile radius (a solution), we do what we can, having taken out one near the house that exhibited the tell-tale galls; these strangely resemble the images of microscopic Covid-19 virus "crowns."

Ash bore is currently in the news, and so we pay particular attention to the two domestic ash trees in the yard. The "bore" is an insect that insinuates itself under the bark, where it insidiously disrupts the circulatory system in the trunk. The beautiful iridescent beetle from China, emerald-colored, likely hopped a ride on a container barge. Arbor Day reports the borer has destroyed at least forty million ash trees in Michigan alone. The use of insecticides, or removal of the tree altogether (and taking care to destroy the wood) remain the two options at present.

Our initial intent was to plant trees all along; this charge (how we viewed it—as part of who we are) would on no account have shrunk to a sad regret. Though in truth, I try to dissuade Jeff from planting additional fruit trees, other than replacements, having more than can be easily tended at present. I foresee hiring pickers as the years unfold; helpers admit they find the task enjoyable. But I digress. Like the root squirming its dark, crawly way through soil, zigzagging along unhurriedly, I acknowledge and consider all possible pathways to meaning.

Our parents, the children's grandparents, and the grandchildren's great-grandparents, are buried far from here. Our roots in them extend deep into the distance. Think of them (roots) as persevering *all* the way from Britain and France, to the Shenandoah Valley, Louisiana, North Carolina, Alabama, and Missouri; to Kansas, Arkansas, Ohio, South Carolina, to Georgia and Casper, Wyoming; at last, to meet up with the memorial

Arborvitaes' shallow root system, anchoring the pair from beneath. Incidentally, a medicinal tea made from the young leaves of this conifer is a traditional remedy for bronchitis and other respiratory ailments. Tree of Life—of breath. Indeed.

Inhabiting a narrow valley as we do, we don't fear the occasional tornado warning, but a mighty wind *could* knock over trees, those with shallow roots. Standing People are *they;* Walking People are *we.* Distant cousins, we share some twenty-five percent of our DNA. For what we lack in familial ties in this rural place, we dwell among trees that (*who!*) greet us each morning, and upon returning from a trip. Ever the sentinels and welcoming monkish porters (attending visitors at the gate), they stand and observe, these silent, unflappable guards. As I inform our young granddaughters, fairies only move when not being observed. *So too the trees?* At least by degrees.

We can only *endeavor* to meet obligations and purposes. A few intertwine. If I stress this notion enough, it may be remembered. Wrens and nuthatches make their nests inside Thuja's shady, safe interior. It's a delight to see one flit out, a living ornament.

Figure 16 The Writing Hut

Figure 17 The Vines After Frost

Figure 18 Honeycrisps and Fireside

s

PENTIMENTO

After Pawpaw died of complications between Huntington's Disease and pneumonia, MoMo continued to live in their gray cottage on Grayson Street, in Charleston Heights, now called North Charleston, lately in the news for an unspeakable tragedy and a president's heartfelt rendition of "Amazing Grace." She lived a short block from the First Baptist Church she attended. Its bells rang on the hour, with a carillon on Sundays to summon the faithful. Momo taught Kindergarten there, and continued to sew for clients and her family. She wouldn't have used the word *client,* referring to them instead as "my ladies." On Christmas Eve, we were permitted to open her handmade gifts of cozy pajamas and robes.

For my wedding, after creating six bridesmaids' dresses (of yellow-checkered gingham), and the Holly Hobby dress and bonnet for our flower girl, Leigh Ann, this remarkable woman confessed relief—the only instance I ever heard her utter a complaint. I believe she would have sewn my wedding dress, had I not found the one I loved in Laramie, a muslin and lace Jessica McClintock, popular at the time, for which I happily paid $36.00. "I couldn't have made it for that," MoMo declared. She was being kind. Of course, she could have, minus the hours of labor. Maybe *I* was practicing kindness? This was in 1974. With inflation, today the dress would have cost $188.00. Frugal, I was.

The dress, slightly yellowed with age, hangs beside my collection of "singing dresses,"—those I performed in, or wore in sisters' weddings—all waiting for granddaughters to play "dress up" in, just as my sisters and I played in the gorgeous gowns my grandmother had made for our mother. Those *shushed* of taffeta and much fancier stuff than mere muslin, but a ball is a ball, while my wedding dress portended a crofter's lifestyle and more practical magic.

How we all managed to fit in my grandparents' house on Grayson Street mystifies me. Love expands space, just as resentment will shrink it. Nine of us could gather around the ample dining table, to copious amounts of food carried from the kitchen in bowls and platters, served in what is now referred to as "family style." A thick plastic cover protected the white table cloth against the certainty of spills by little eaters. Sunday dinner included both her fried chicken *and* ham; field peas from her parents' garden in Alabama; mashed potatoes *and* sweet potatoes; biscuits and gravy. MoMo produced fig preserves (a favorite!) from fruit picked in the backyard, where we *chilluns* formed mud pies, played kitchen with cast-off pots and pans, and avoided the red ants. Unsuccessfully once, as brother André painfully learned.

We made regular trips over the years and were thrilled to visit either Folly Beach or Isle of Palms. Much sand found its way between the sheets of our floor pallets. Dad had rounded up six lengths of foam rubber so we wouldn't have to sleep on the hard floor of the tiny parlor and dining room. He and Mom took the second bedroom, once shared by the sisters. We all shared the one bathroom. It was a matter of logistics—my father's area of expertise.

The house was small but cozy, and MoMo's love and cooking made it another home. Between the smell of Coppertone and fried chicken, my senses found Nirvana. As we'd normally visit during the summer (*the beach! the beach!*), at night we could get by with only a sheet and a pillow in the humid heat. I retain a fading *pentimento* of the fetid smell wafting over her neighborhood and indoors; hot and sticky, old—the very Earth and her sea—mingling with that of the paper mill and its sulfur fumes. I associate all of it with MoMo, with love, and accented by the Avon hand creams her students were forever presenting her.

Somehow, we children knew we couldn't be rambunctious in that space. Fortunately, the grade-school playground waited around the corner. In those days, we could be let out the door (or kicked out)—as long as we older siblings understood our responsibility—to keep an eye out.

Once upon a time, an angel-haired boy named Richard lived across the street from my grandparents. I have a photograph of us as toddlers, taken on Easter Sunday in the front yard. In the picture, we are beaming for the camera. Richard wears a suit and bow tie, and I'm in a starched dress with petticoats. The angel-haired boy contracted polio and spent several years in an iron lung before succumbing to the disease. I visited him one day when we were in town, soon after we returned from France in 1961. He turned his bright eyes and shining forehead to me and smiled. The "iron lung" contraption he was obliged to lie in looked like a long gray tin can with no label. Only his head protruded from one end. I felt uncomfortable, but in retrospect, was it pity? Sorrow? Imagine how he felt. *Ra-churd* (how MoMo pronounced his name) *is sweet on you,* she had once told me. In that early photograph, we are holding hands. Is that all it took?

Blessings, Richard, wherever you are. No one dies, it is said, who is remembered with kindness. May it be.

Our beach days, as stated, were passed either at Folly Beach or the Isle of Palms. The latter, once linked by a long-long bridge, is now reached by the Isle of Palms Connector Bridge. The scene reads like so many summer-vacation tropes: one station wagon, filled to the gills with plastic float donuts; buckets, shovels, spoons; plus, mounds of towels and gleeful kids. I don't remember a cooler or umbrella—the current accouterments to such an outing. I do recall the cherry-red and white Thermos, holding two gallons of Kool-Aid. Ours was "the basic package." A couple of webbed, folding chairs for the adults completed the gear.

All our senses were engaged and charged to maximum capacity by these outings. Jumping through salty waves with our father was about the most fun I think we all had together. Pure joy. A child's delight triples when genuinely shared by such parental participation. He would throw us up and into a coming wave. How we thrilled at the play! Mom, by contrast, never cared for the water and hadn't learned to swim. As a fixed *life guard* of sorts, she sun-bathed, surveilled and smoked her Pall Malls. Her idea of Heaven, no doubt. Sunshine showed an affinity for her and she turned dark most summers, never burning—like the rest of us did. *Solarcaine* helped.

Folly Beach boasted a midway with carousel and Ferris wheel. Hawkers too. The two public beaches were literally twenty-four miles apart, but much further in atmosphere. It took longer to drive to the island, but Dad preferred its pristine quality. He was more adamant than Mom. Unaware of how she felt much of the time (she kept her own counsel), I believe she was haunted by water, to paraphrase Norman Maclean's words. The prospect of a sand-filled car, and later, gritty bedsheets (despite baths for everyone) may have dampened her excitement, but I've discovered there is little more rewarding than watching one's family thoroughly enjoying themselves. The *full catastrophe,* as Zorba the Greek says, is indeed that. A fullness of being, careening toward the inevitable.

MoMo wouldn't accompany us on these forays. She stayed home to cook and set her home to rights, I suspect. She later sold the house and Mom and I helped her move back to Andalusia, Alabama, to her father's corner lot, where she had a mobile home set up.

She cared for him, our sometimes-cranky great-grandfather, until he died.

MoMo's health declined quickly. She lived with our parents after Alzheimer's presented and, when it was time, she was moved to a nursing home, to die soon after. Thoroughly worn out. I regret our children not having known her when she was herself—a giver. In all ways.

When I visit beaches, my soul longs for sounds of screeching laughter over the crashing waves and calling sea gulls. A distinct smell of fish too. Pure, unadulterated nostalgia, I admit. Quiet beaches have their place, but it's another experience altogether. Serious. Contemplative. *Lonesome?*

We incur debts we can never repay. To our parents and grandparents. For the gift of themselves. In the throes of young adulthood, life comes too fast to sort it out, to read between the lines, to pay the strictest attention. I hope for a forgiving reckoning from my ancestors, that their selfless love and unsung devotion may be paid forward. I must believe it can be. No one gets out alive, as our son texted the other day, but in the meantime . . . it's all a day at the beach.

AUTUMN II

If "first frost" honors the traditional date, by the Fall Equinox we should see utterly deflated winter squash greens spread like languid strands of seaweed over the garden. The buttercup variety is our favorite, as it tastes the sweetest and keeps well enough. These near globes must be "hardened off," meaning, left in the sun for a few days after they have been harvested. A curing process, much like allowing garlic to hang.

In consulting Jeff's tidy daily agenda, I'm reminded of his industrious bent—and recall what jobs fit the season. Only "a hand" in certain enterprises, I would not expect him to sit beside me in my writing cabin, compose sentences and/or type my thoughts. Besides, he is the "hunt and peck" type. I typed most of his papers at university. We do consult on chore procedures, however, and he will proof the salient chapters herein. The man is a work horse. *Which?* you ask. More of a light breed—certainly not a Clydesdale. Quarter Horse, maybe.

September 9 entry (not officially Autumn, but relevant): *Trimmed hail-damaged grapes on lower vines*. For the next day, after noting his early-morning temperature record (forty-eight degrees), and the sky as "clear and hazy," I read (?), *Cleaned and organized shop bench* [Halleluiah!]. Fall can be rainy, and on the eleventh day of that month, he recorded .7 inches in the plastic amber gauge (fastened, recall, to the top of the fence, near the cattleguard). Jeff also noted he had misread the bedside clock, to rise at two-thirty in the morning, believing it was five a.m., his usual Rise and Shine. I see he cleaned out the gutters on that day; *between storms*, he wrote. The next day, Cody arrived to help with a project. Our go-to help when we need more expertise, we thank heaven for him and his affable willingness. Our acquaintance began when he was eight years old and his family moved to the area. Cody's a good carpenter and plumber, two useful occupations in a rural area. He and Jeff re-plumbed and installed a new water heater, *in case*. It wouldn't do to have the current one break down at an inauspicious time; it was old. Practicing preventive maintenance is not to be mocked. Especially in rustic America.

The twenty-third of September had Jeff building a dog house for the new pup, Gabe. Several members of the Amish community arrived to pick grapes at $1.25 a pound. On Saturdays, members of the colony can be found outside the local grocery store until the weather changes, selling their goods. Once, after picking, several jars of grape jam and jelly appeared that weekend on their sale table. I also put up preserves, much of it to give as gifts.

A neighbor's son helped us last year. We harvested the rest of the grapes and sold several pounds to a farmers' market in Spearfish, where Jeff is renowned as "The Garlic Guy." Apple harvest must wait for frost, which coincided with "first freeze" this year. Tricky, guessing when apples are at risk. It's a-seat-of-the-pants decision; intuition and gut feeling. Celebrating harvest time is an exercise in mindfulness and acknowledgment of generosity. *"The desire to celebrate is the longing to enter more deeply into the mystery of actuality,"* wrote the late John O'Donohue in *Eternal Echoes: Celtic Reflections on Our Yearning to Belong.* In spring, as we celebrate the orchard bloom, we might also assign the latent intention to further anticipate and rejoice in the crop—like neo parents around the birth of their first child.

On a bright, sunshiny day in early October, crisp and invigorated by radiant heat from our very own star, Ivan helped us harvest twelve bushels of apples and haul firewood. We protect the neat wood pile with a large tarp against rain and snow—which brings me to these "uncertain times," as they are being called.

I debate mention of the present chaos, to wit, the falling economies, the Covid-19 pandemic, the changing climate, and worldwide political unrest. A mouthful of dust and ashes, all of it. But when I consider my reasons for this manual (and memoir), I feel a shiver down my spine, with respect to purpose. In wishing to create what may serve as a map for our children (irrespective of their decision to spend more time here), I quickly revised the notion to include *anyone* who might find themselves in a similar lifestyle situation, never mind where (though location would make a difference to the details).

Today the news cycles once again report horrendous statistics and painful realizations, and each morning I awake conscious of a world in upheaval. The tide has turned, and not merely so. A tsunami threatens—a tidal wave of woe. Could it transform us like raw gemstones tossed into a rock tumbler, in too-facile analogy? Living sanely on the Earth, with renewed respect and purpose, will require and entail a more profound epistemology and appreciation of the land: how to defend the planet, work with her systems and, finally, *for* her. Listening more attentively to aggrieved parties in the world, with "the ear of the heart," as Saint Benedict suggests, is just as crucial. Peace follows justice. It seems we're all still grains of sand in the oyster, evolutionarily speaking.

The present age is being hailed the *Anthrópocene,* with emphasis on how humanity has altered the course of species and the Earth herself. Elizabeth Kolbert's Pulitzer winner, *The Sixth Extinction, An Unnatural History,* is hardly escapist literature, but strangely comforting, despite well-researched studies designed to keep you awake at night. No, really—wouldn't you rather enter the future with eyes wide open? With a clue? With hope? I came away feeling more pragmatic than ever. And determined. At least more aware. I wish to grasp the dynamics and repercussions, at least insofar as I am able.

When I read about the symptoms associated with the Covid-19 virus, i.e., difficulty in catching one's breath and hypoxia, landing many on ventilators in order to simply breathe, I hear the Earth whisper: *"Now do you understand how I struggle to breathe as well? My lungs—the forests—are being decimated every day. Now do you see? I choke on pollution, too. What will it take, child?"*

Rather than create a radical's manifesto to accompany this homestead manual and memoir, I take up my original intent, by way of personal Field Notes, in a yin-yang balance of duty and observation. I take the tortoise tack, to keep on keepin' on, in equanimity, *letting the low side drag,* as they say, meaning, "This is a disaster; I'm depressed about it. I let it drag behind me and keep on going," to *allow* it. It somehow belongs here at this particular time in history. I've heard it phrased as *letting the rough side drag.* Feeling rough is British for sick. But onward! As friend Shirley encourages—to good effect, recalling Churchill's advice, "If you're going through hell, *keep going!"*

- The "Apples 4 Sale" sign, placed beside the mailbox, attracts interest. Use it.

- Continue to harvest apples. We fill bags and deliver them to neighbors.

- Dig root crops: carrots, beets, horseradish, potatoes—if more remain.

- Plant garlic after tilling and raking half the garden. (We practice crop rotation here; the following year, plant the other side.) Plow the rows with a hoe, carving a four or five-inch trough the length of the patch; break apart the saved-back heads of garlic (the largest specimens), and press single cloves into the soil, pointy-end up, every hand-width apart. Pull the soil back over and tamp. Water if necessary. Fall rains are usually sufficient. Like the tulip, the garlic bulb requires all of winter's forces to coax its brand of magic. A rule of thumb has us wait until after the full moon in October to plant the cloves, when the phase encourages root growth. But do get them in the ground anytime, if constrained by the calendar.

- Juicing the Dalgo crabs ensures a gorgeous ruby-red liquid for jellies, one of our favorites. This apple tree grows behind the house, near the blue well cover.

- Jeff is experimenting with the Frontenac and Marechal Foch varietals. Time will tell if the wine turns out.

- Mow lawn, possibly for the last time.

A yearly Apple Pressing (alas, not in 2020) presents an opportunity to gather neighbors, and everyone carries home a container of cider. Generally, the ratio is one bushel for one gallon of liquid. This is a good time to invite farther-afield friends who stay for the weekend, making it a house-party occasion. The help of many hands harkens back to barn-raisings, on a much smaller scale. Last year, shoulder pain prevented my sharing the burden, but I kept everyone in Irish coffee and snacks. And cider, of course. They were appreciative.

We feed the too-spoiled apples to the deer. As we seldom use pesticides (and never in the orchard), a fair number of fruits become feasts for wasps and birds. Deer have learned to expect the fragrant apple treat, and it's a hoot to watch the fawns vying for "a place at the table." We are unwitting voyeurs to mating habits, as bucks chase away competitors. Because we have successfully fenced out any deer from orchard and garden all these years, we owe them a taste for enduring the sweet smell of fruit all season from a distance.

If we do have an "Indian Summer," it comes and goes like a nostalgic performance from an aging Broadway star, dressed in yards of lace and fading frippery. Snow falls more regularly now. Jeff's entry for November 6 reads, *Snowed all day. Racked wine.*

On Hunting

On the first day of deer season, November 1, Jeff and I register the near and distant *booms!* Of gunfire in our valley, much as one might hear an old grandfather clock's chime, cycling time. Area ranches permit hunting, for the most part. Friends and family arrive to answer an ancient call and celebrate a true Harvest Home, or in the case of spring turkey season, the return of warmer weather. Just as poignant and welcome.

The Hunt addresses an ancient question: that of hunger. It has come to be associated with sport, however, and, never an apologist for trophy hunting, I believe the game biologists are good at what they do regarding game management. Using the meat, and the hide, if possible, answer a moral question. Neither of us have taken an animal in years, but our son (normally) returns each year to hunt. Jeff helps him butcher as part of the responsibility, and John has become adept at preparing game in recipes. It's good meat. If you're not vegetarian. And it impacts global warming far less than beef.

Some specify the entire state as "frontier," further removed from mere *rural*, hence, game abounds in our county. Multiple species of fish, including walleye, as well. I once heard someone "highly suggest" the construction of a wall around the entire state to keep it pristine. This would mess with herd migration, however, and not be particularly helpful. Thanks to our open spaces and sparse population, hunting of white-tail and mule deer, turkeys, geese, ducks, pronghorn antelope, and elk is closely regulated through the Wyoming Game and Fish Department, to promote and sustain the health of the species. (Yes, the upshot is not lost on me.) Mountain lions and coyotes, as predators (like us), are treated differently, through a management program. Presently, the big cats and coyotes are considered fair game, if deemed a threat, existential or not. My own view on cougars depends on their distance and intention. When we kept horses and sheep, I would have defended them from a prowling cat, to be sure.

Sage grouse populations are falling, an issue of concern to those who would prefer the species' survival.

When I was eleven, my father took me dove hunting. I still have the 4-10 shotgun I used, now at the ready against rattlers and other varmints. Mom always roasted the birds, with rice and gravy. I didn't hunt again until Jeff and I were first married and we needed a more economical food source, being cash-strapped newlyweds. Hunting provided us with venison and antelope, ducks and geese, and, myriad bonding experiences. I took my first deer near Casper Mountain, at 400-plus yards. Dad always said we dove-hunt to practice for the next shot. It just took a while for my next shot.

Rites of passage notwithstanding for a kid, or anyone who feels a deep connection to the circle of life (an *I eat you, now you eat me* sort of thing), I believe we owe our integrity the bare facts of our nourishment, and its origin—even vegans, à propos the plant people. Perhaps I do write a manifesto of sorts, perhaps not. That our son can provide meat for his family, from a purely bedrock manner (no reference to cavemen— rather, as a fundamental talent) gives me a measure of peace and, yes, pride.

In 1978, Jeff and I drew an elk license. A boon! Except for my being seven months pregnant with our daughter at the time of the hunt. We borrowed the old Alaskan camper from Jeff's father and headed for the hunt area in the near center of Wyoming. As luck would have it, we filled on the first day out. I say "we," as it was a concerted effort in my view. Once home, the large cow elk took us eighteen hours straight to butcher in our small kitchen.

The weather prevented our hanging the carcass outdoors for any length of time. We had once learned that painful lesson. I will never forget the writhing swarm of maggots that "spontaneously generated" on an elk quarter given to us by a friend when we lived in Cheyenne. We had hung it in a too-warm room off our kitchen, resulting in a terrible loss.

Those not acquainted with meat processing might be appalled, envisioning a right bloody mess, but it's not like that at all. Once the carcass has cooled out (and thankfully, this one had), and with the valuable assistance of one of my cookbooks that show cuts of meat, we simply sharpened filet knives and saws and dove in. My job mostly entailed cutting the fascia connective tissue from the muscle—basically sliding the long blade between the two, and dropping the tissue in the trash can.

It was our first elk, wonderful meat, and we were more than grateful.

Now a conversation I need to have, regarding firearms: I contend that certain guns are suitable on a homestead. However, I distinguish between rifles, shotguns, and pistols used for hunting and protection (being isolated and living among badgers, snakes, and cougars), and those military-grade weapons that are horrifically used against school children, congregations, concert goers, and protesters. Further, Wyoming reports the highest per capita suicide-by-gun statistic in the country. Two-thirds of suicides, 114, were by firearm in 2019. A newly established hotline number for the state is **1-800-273-8255.** Nation-wide, it's **988.**

The subject of gun legislation riles many in the United States, but I believe the salient questions are being glossed over and ignored. My husband proposes a designation on one's driver's license, or a similar document, contingent on certain criteria, including a background check with psychological assessment. Unfortunately, if some poor devil is hellbent on destruction, he will find a way and regulation be damned.

So many ills of society hang on a simple solution. Caring for our brothers and sisters, and learning to forgive ourselves and one another—an Occam's Razor of a remedy—simplest is best.

Amid hunting guests, football on television, and battening down proverbial hatches, Jeff finds plenty to occupy his time in autumn. A recurring task in late fall is the *Echinacea* dig. Our youngest granddaughter accompanied him one year and proved an enthusiastic assistant. Later, I showed her how to fill a jar twice— once with root pieces, then with the alcohol—to extract the healing properties of the plant. I use the cut-up *Echinacea* roots to make tinctures against flu and cold symptoms (if a secondary respiratory infection presents), and to strengthen the overall immune system. It's a favorite preventive against infection. I have an auto-immune malady, and myself, take this herb only on rare occasions.

In later chapters I include several herbal remedies, as well as family recipes. Making medicines is a fulfilling activity—including salves, tinctures, herbal vinegars, and honeys. One of my treasures is a small library of herbals, modern grimoires of rich, green blessings.

My own schedule is governed by whatever writing task(s) I have, but seasonal jobs and obligations wildly wave their hands and I have several candidates from which to choose. This is how a schematic chart of enthusiasms may serve, in order to judge where attention might best be focused. I suspect it depends on how desperate you are to keep track of Every Little Thing. For my part, a running inspection keeps me from feeling fragmented. Still, "at loose ends" occasionally describes my mood. I'm learning to accept, if not welcome, these *spirits,* and nourish them by idly leafing through a magazine, or by sitting outdoors, gazing, and doing nothing, or by staring at a fire. The "not doing" is the *doing.* The herbalist and author Susun Weed calls it, *Serenity Medicine,* Step Zero in her Seven Medicines protocol. I'm sadly aware of unintended consequences in throwing off routine altogether, vacations notwithstanding, and keep one eye peeled, as it were.

Routine, one source suggests, comes from the word for route, or way. I respectfully disagree. I believe it comes from the French word for wheel, or *roue* (from which the word for route came). Think of a pie chart. Picture your pie, say, apple, with measured concentric circles radiating from the center. I believe that everyone (whether they know it or not) holds fast to certain important areas in their lives, i.e., family, occupation, and health. I count writing as my work, but include necessary tasks to maintain our "living" here, ergo, the myriad seasonal chores. To resume my pie chart illustration, music practice claims a slice, as does serving nonprofit associations, but most important, in maintaining friendships and familial ties. À propos Braeburn Croft, it's also the name of my publishing imprint, ergo, I add publisher, after writer.

The most endearing occupations cleave to the center. I employ the mercenary word as it is used in French: *s'occuper de*—to take care of—while less esteemed yet important cares appear further afield as I shamelessly assign values to roles. But my circle is never meant to divide inside from outside, as though everything beyond is somehow irrelevant, i.e., "outer reaches of the universe." The abstract serves as an organizing principle. And so now, let's spring to the use of the encircling spiral. . . .

The iconic image has been depicted for thousands of years. I would love to learn its original intent, lost in pre-history. In 1999, my daughter and I viewed such an image carved onto stone, measuring about one-and-a-half feet in diameter. Discovered deep within a paleolithic mound off the Gulf of Morbihan in Brittany, the image appeared at the end of a long tunnel where the singular light of a solstice sun would penetrate the dark distance. Sadly, we missed the auspicious date and made do with electric light.

Spirals spoke to the nascent consciousness of early women and men. Archeologists and anthropologists excavating an ancient settlement called Skara Brae, in Scotland's Orkney Isles, unearthed the symbol I've adopted as imprint and personal logo. It speaks to me. This is what it whispers: *"I am the original womb. See my breasts, swelling in response to an infant's need and the people's nourishment. Fire burns in my head above, and smolders in my womb below. Spirit and matter as One. All is One."*

Symbols may see in the dark, suggests the Celtic mystic, John O'Donahue. Where our roots abide.

A ZEN OF HEART SENSE

Here I distill a still life of a living, its elements scattershot on a divine banquet table by a capricious creator. What to choose in the telling? When considering which props to include in a painting, we are taught to choose carefully, to be discriminating, to practice discernment. My art professor once raised his eyebrows in disbelief the first time I tried to incorporate every assorted object in my day's drawing. When had I missed *that* instruction? To be choosy. To examine options and capacities. To practice the art of quality over quantity. So too, my "swollen appetites" required edits. (And not *a little* humility.) Music, I need, however, as in "How Can I Keep from Singing?" From a repertoire spanning fifty-five years, which song to sing? Which new one to learn by heart? The Zen would have me play with a steely-eyed vision, a forest-versus-trees dialectic, while the writing demands an overall truth. My efforts at expression fulfill a longing for heart-sense. More on music later.

Speaking of the heart, and all that enriches it (especially a life partner), *The American College Dictionary* defines husbandry as: 1. the business of a farmer; agriculture; farming. 2. careful or thrifty management; frugality; thrift. 3. the management of domestic affairs, or of resources generally.

After thirty years in education, husbanding students as teacher, principal, and superintendent, my husband continues to seek and find joy in gardening and tending an orchard. It would yet be called a *simple* life if modern technologies (such as the Internet and satellite television) didn't figure. NPR might have sufficed once, but the times demand an informed citizenry as part of husbandry's management obligations. Too, our relative isolation is mitigated with well-considered television series, films, documentaries and sports events. The twenty-four-hour news cycle serves as an obnoxious kind of early warning system. Comedy alleviates existential dread, as antidote, when little in the world today may be considered a laughing matter. But I digress. Fortunately for us both, a gift for husbandry, whether by educating school children or gardening, defines my "retired" husband more than any one characteristic. Hailing from a long line of farmers on his mother's side, Jeff is more Samuel than Carrier (in my opinion). The following speaks to synchronicity *and* roots:

Our son has wound up in the Midwest, not far from the childhood home of Frank and Jesse James in Kearney, Missouri. During a visit one year, our family decided to tour the infamous home, now a museum. A few weeks before, I had discovered a strange twist in Jeff's ancestry. As it happens, while I was confirming the date of his mother's death online, up popped a website with further information about her family, the Samuels, and their ancestry. Seems Jeff's great-great-great Uncle Reuben Samuel, a physician, was the stepfather of the James brothers.

One day in 1863, during the Civil War, a troop of Union soldiers arrived at the farm in Kearney searching for Frank James, who had already made a name for himself by stealing monies from the "Yanks." Jesse, busy tilling a field, was apprehended and whipped for his stubborn silence. Dr. Samuel fared worse. He was hanged three times as persuasion, with the third try landing him in the St. Joseph, Missouri sanatorium, suffering from brain damage. He did not survive long. Accounts differ as to whether he gave up his stepson's whereabouts. Folks in Kearney are proprietary regarding their famous resident, and quick to defend Jesse's actions, in light of the horrors he'd experienced during the war. One author suggested the kid used his stepfather's treatment and the Confederate fervor to justify his raids and robberies. Another article cites his "skewed moral code." When the famous Pinkerton Agency tossed an incendiary device into the Samuel-James home, Jesse's mother, Zerelda James Samuel, was maimed, and his half-brother Archie perished in the explosion. History judges on weighted scales.

Jeff's sister recalls a time their mother scolded them for rough play, exclaiming, "You might *think* you're related to Jesse James, but you aren't!" The knowledge that he was related to the James brothers (by marriage— I hasten to add) entertained and fascinated for a while, with family members sending us National Geographic editions on the hapless youth.

What's this to do with husbandry? Not a thing— except for Reuben Samuel's relatives yanking up their Missouri roots and decamping to Arkansas, where they continued to farm in the Pea Ridge area. And it's a good story.

In 1759, another John Carrier arrived in the American Colonies from Westminster, England to settle in the Shenandoah Valley. His son fought in the Revolutionary War for the Continentals. The lineage may be further traced to Tennessee, Ohio, then Kansas, where Jeff's grandmother Shelby saved her egg money and purchased an eighty-acre wheat field, known ever after as "The Kansas Farm." This was in 1919, before women secured their right to vote (an *inalienable* right, truth be told, and not a privilege to be granted by any one segment of society). One could acquire a tract of land for chicken feed, but inheritance laws favored the husband. I wonder if it was Shelby's husband or Shelby who wanted to have a nest egg, in case.

For decades the wheat has been farmed by the same family, who share the sale proceeds with we absentee owners. Which makes us sharecroppers, I suppose.

Jeff's father believed in land and its capacity for taking care of its caretakers. A sacred contract, so to speak, but one my husband wouldn't necessarily subscribe to, the charge being more an innate—and therefore mostly subconscious—quality.

Jeff manages the Kansas state taxes and fertilizer costs and, after the farmer exacts his share for combining, etcetera, Jeff frets over the best time to sell the remaining crop, a gamble every year, given the market.

This morning we dug potatoes before I settled into my writing time. Generally, we wait until after frost to harvest the spuds, but gardening presupposes dealing with pests. The pesky bug variety. We had planted thirteen short rows of Norland reds, and white Yukons. A friend had shared some of his seed stock and suggested a different horticultural method: plant the seed potatoes at four inches, in shallower trenches than we had in the past, then mound the soil over the growing plant little by little. Which Jeff did do—and there grew healthy, tall aerial stems and leaves. One day I noticed blister beetles on several plants and Jeff picked them off, but too late. Two days later an infestation stripped the greening stalks. (The beetles also like the elderberry bush flowers. *Bah! Humbug!)* It was time to harvest, and the potatoes would be stunted.

Happily, that side of the kitchen garden is partly shaded in the morning, but digging and bending over to gather the crop makes for a tedious chore. Two can accomplish it so much more easily. As with much in life.

The third week of August in 2020 brought high temperatures and we needed rain. The county issued a "red flag" warning. Wild fires from lightning strikes, or resulting from human activity, pose a danger this time of year. A spark from a running tractor can ignite a field and torch a rancher's crop of newly stacked hay. A carelessly tossed cigarette from a moving vehicle will find ample fuel to blacken borrow pits beside the highway—and worse.

When a fire is reported on a neighbor's place (and if we get word), my husband hustles out to help, an unspoken ethic in play. One instance occurred a few years ago just east of us, on the west-facing adjoining ridge. A neighbor's water truck provided the saving grace to douse the area. It was a matter of positioning the vehicle ridge-top and unrolling the heavy hose downhill to the hot spot and firefighters. The same year, a field caught fire on a neighbor's place (sparked by a tractor) and area volunteers showed up with willing hearts, shovels, and grit. I provided drinking water. My physiology at this stage disallows my participation among the fighting ranks, but several young women worked alongside the men and I am in grateful awe of them all. It's downright hot, dirty, and exhausting work, judging by Jeff's appearance whenever he returns from a fire.

Husbandry, you may have gathered, is not limited to bucolic scenes of eight-foot-tall corn in one's garden, or happy lambs cavorting in a field. It shares a meaningful notion with housewifery, if I may draw an analogy. A Google search defines housewifery similarly to husbandry's third definition, regarding the management of domestic affairs and resources. Each is served by a nourishing and "doing" mindset—*nurturing,* if you will. In a *Quora* online post, Sara Matthews, a language arts teacher, examines what it means to nourish, nurture, *and* cultivate:

"*Nourish* is to supply food. It can be used in poetic manner: Music nourishes my spirit. *Nurture* is to care for—most often used with children—You must nurture your talents so they may thrive and grow. *Cultivate* is to tend, with the intention of fostering growth—cultivate your garden and it will provide you with fruits and vegetables."

Cultivate your life and it will provide you with metaphorical fruits and veggies. You reap what you sow, in other words, no pun intended. Here I must include a darker use of the word, "just to get it out of the way," as my father used to say. My example is his: "She's cultivating you," he once suggested, regarding a certain person's interest in me, possibly feigned. Not meant to be positive, I suspect the tradecraft he learned at the Defense Department, else he simply read a lot of Jean Le Carré. *Toss the dogma and go straight for well-being. Pay attention!* is the lesson I prefer to take away. I am reminded to go cultivate the soil beside the beets, carrots, and marigolds this afternoon, so they may better absorb water. *Well-being will out.* And, prepare your own "soil."

The Water Bearer of the constellation Aquarius suggests a person, male or female—depending on the culture and source—eternally pouring water from a large urn upon the earth and her environs. It speaks to the Absolute in relative terms. What is also needed in a desperately thirsty world? Kind husbandry, wise housewifery and torrents of grace, a *Heart*-sense.

A ZEN OF HEART SENSE II, Taproots

E*quus caballus*

Two constants in my peripatetic life have been music and horses, the fancy modifier reserved for the first thirty-four years of multiple moves. Like *The Wizard of Oz,* opening in somber sepia tones, then, *Surprise!* a technicolor Oz, my paltry, two-dimensional words on the page may render scant evidence of "living color"—how NBC illustrated the advent of color television. The realization is as much acceptance as discovery. Surprise, surprise.

What lends a life color? Near my first home in Alexandria, Virginia, "the pony man" set up his rides, essentially a round exercise manège with several shaggy Shetlands, each tethered to the end of a bar, like spokes on a wheel, fastened to a central rotating pole. A May pole. Pony Man walked alongside me—likely at my parents' request. Too young for perfect memory, I believe I internalized a sensation associated with riding: pure joy. Later in France, while visiting Nice with our neighbor, Monsieur Chèvrier, five-year-old *moi* rode on a donkey, led by an old Frenchman with stubbled cheeks, cigarette ever dangling from his mouth. He was wearing a beret, naturally. The photograph shows me grinning ear to ear, and looking back over my shoulder to my father, the photographer. Another time, Dad lifted me high upon a staid Percheron, the tallest animal I'd ever seen up close. By then I had learned who Joan of

Arc was, and that she'd likely ridden one of these great horses into battle.

Smitten by sweet association, music and the artful poignancy of The Horse became entwined.

The day before school starts up in France signals a *jour de fête*, or holiday, in villages, for returning students and their families. Traditionally, it includes a carnival, with a swing ride and a *manège*, or carousel. Happy music blared from a mounted loudspeaker as I clung to the painted pony pole, rising, falling, and whirring round and round, to lean for the prize dangling from a hook, awarding another ride. Today I wonder if the grab-it game is deemed too dangerous. We grow over-protective of one risk and not nearly enough of another.

Christmas celebrations in France are magical, especially for the children. I risk sounding overly sentimental, but consider my theory: whether you are religious, spiritual, agnostic, or atheist, an ancient imperative to mark the season(s) bubbles in our DNA. Even if one is atheist, the exception proves the rule, and protesting too much tells a tale. All creation is programmed to honor rhythms and respect significance. Observing nature (in both senses) remains our simplest sanctuary, in order to "bind back to that which is greater," the original meaning of religion.

My parents observed the French traditions of Noël as well as possible, including the *Réveillon* meal taken after Midnight Mass. The word means, beautifully, "The Awakening."

That year the decorated tree sparkled with colored lights and tinsel in the dining room. Framed outdoors in the large window, the magical sight burst mine and my brother's young sensibilities. After the meal, Dad told me to go look under the tree for a large wrapped gift. He gestured to it. It measured twenty-four by thirty-six inches. I must have looked perplexed as he told me to bring it into the parlor (these were not "living rooms"). I did as I was told and he said, "Open it, Sugar." I did and came face to face with a mighty steed's head. By the look in the horse's eyes, the flaring nostrils and the heavy bit, this was a stallion, running hell bent for leather, as we say. The matted and framed drawing, colored with pencils, was signed by the artist. Dad had bought it from the local antique dealer in Moret-sur-Loing. I loved it immediately—more so as a gift from my father. Like his mother before him, he knew how to encourage and nurture the passions of even the youngest among us. When else is more appropriate? He showed a rare gift for giving all his life.

Today the artwork hangs in our guest room. The image of a charging horse, head-on, is too intense for my husband, who has graciously accepted my penchant for horses. I bless the forbearance.

Back in the States, I took riding lessons at the adjacent Army base stables. A year later, when I was ten, a sixteen-hand palomino named Paavo came into my life. Dad thought it amusing the horse's name was his (Paul) in the Finnish and Estonian languages. Paavo and I suffered a couple of mishaps, and I learned my lessons (as usual) the hard way.

My parents had asked me to ride Paavo to our quarters on the base, about a mile away. Mom wanted pictures made of her wearing her riding habit. She had taken lessons in Alabama, but now lacked the time to pursue her interest(s). I, on the other hand, resembled a squire's page, hair cut in said style, jeans, jodhpur boots, oxford shirt tucked in, beguiling smile. Photos made, I mounted and reined Paavo across the street to the open hillside. Truth be told, I felt a trifle triumphant about it all—this pride soon to be squashed. Paavo became frightened, then fidgety, and then he bolted in the direction of the stables at a mad dash, with terrified me clutching and pulling on the reins. How I managed to stay seated, God only knows; I don't. At the busy highway (I *still* see it), with cars passing left and right, Paavo abruptly halted at the curb. I did not go over his head into the traffic. I'm still here.

Heart firmly squeezed in throat, I pulled his head away and he ambled slowly back to our house; I was not processing information very well. And *then* I received a brutal tongue-lashing from a horsey neighbor who scolded me for not knowing how to turn a runaway. Mind, I was ten years old. She showed me and I've remembered to use the heated instruction several times. Mostly, I remember feeling mortified for my parents. I'd humiliated them—not to mention the obvious.

For those who are interested, and depending on which direction is open, you reach forward, keeping your seat (heels down!), then, as close to the bit as you can manage, pull the rein outward (not back) to turn the horse's head. Make tighter and tighter circles. Your mount will slow.

When Dad was transferred from North Carolina to Georgia—his last assignment—they asked a friend to haul Paavo down, surprising me. We stabled him at a small barn near our house. Mom, ever determined to make it work, bought a sorrel Welsh pony named Bill, as company for Paavo. Then came Cloudy, a gray Shetland. My siblings felt less attracted to horses, and the ponies were eventually sold. Sadly, the camaraderie at the base stables I had been a part of, horse-crazy kids who took lessons and rode together, did not translate for my brother and sisters at the isolated new location.

The property owner informed Mom one day that miscreants were mistreating Paavo by throwing things at him. My frightened horse responded in kind, by growing mean-spirited. It was beyond my ken and broke my heart. In the end, he was traded for a bay quarter horse named Black Jack. Who reared. A lot. We finally sold him after he ran away with me and my brother André, who was riding double behind me. The forest road near the property prevented my being able to turn him as my horsey neighbor once showed me, but Black Jack finally slowed, and that was the end of that for a few years.

At fourteen, I joined a Mounted Drill Team (horse provided), the concept similar to the Royal Canadian Mounted Police troop, theirs described as "Power, Precision and Poetry on Horseback." Sixteen strong, we were The High Noon Paraders. Area horseshows booked us. My mother, and our sponsor, Mrs. Bradshaw, arranged a bus tour for us (and a few others) to go see Expo '67 in Montreal. At the last minute, Mom cancelled her trip, probably having to do with Dad's health. I never learned the reason and she never showed disappointment.

It was a whirlwind extravaganza of silly hotel-room high jinks and the making of disgusting concoctions for our team leader to drink. For money. She was a wild-child. Perhaps she just needed the money. One hotel room was trashed, I remember. I was appalled, mystified and embarrassed by the behavior—an early lesson in mob behavior. Why would anyone want to make life harder for anyone? But that's what they did. And what I've done from time to time. It is what we *all* do as maladaptive humans. But Expo '67 was grand. I bought carved chess pieces in the Russian pavilion for my parents.

Upon our return, an opportunity to acquire a bay mare for $125 presented itself. (This *was* 1967.) Bay Rum was a sweet thing. A quarter-horse-thoroughbred cross, she was well trained and we enjoyed long hours together. The stable's owners also permitted me to show their dappled gray Arabian stallion, Halali Navy Blue. He was a dream and I fell in love with the breed, understanding why the Bedouins might share a tent with their horses. Another member of the drill team showed a second stud in Arabian costume classes. I envied the romance of her exotic clothing, and that one of the requirements of the class was a gallop around the arena, the rider's head dress and cape whipping behind her.

After my father's auto accident, when our family had to leave quickly for Louisiana, I left Bay Rum behind. She was ultimately handed over to the owners of the stables in return for several months' board. A second *last* thing my mother needed at that hectic time was yet another obligation, personal or financial. My younger brother and sisters responded to the move with excitement, cheerfulness and, I dare say, hope—even if this quality was unspoken or unconscious. I recall feeling proud and relieved for their resilience, if not identifying it as such.

For eighteen years I shared a home with my younger siblings, and I regret not having been more present to them. This may be a common source of remorse and sadness, and I note it with that overweening sense of Catholic guilt you hear about. Loath to shrive myself here, I would instead express my admiration and love to these, my "first children," for whom I was often responsible. When I behaved aloof and detached, away in a world of my own making, I beg forgiveness. Our second childhoods lie before us in which to settle accounts. We remain bookends of our lives.

By the time we returned to Georgia from Louisiana, I had grown ambivalent about many interests, except for playing my guitar and singing. As a lifeline and means of expression, music indeed soothed, whereas riding had spoken mainly to my physical side. But it's all one, and, as I often say, comparisons are odious . . . and Mom wasn't through with me yet.

Now working nights delivering babies at the nearby hospital, Mom's LPN asked if I'd be interested in showing her palomino stud in English classes. I agreed. After school, I drove the ten miles to their property to ride, travelling to horseshows most weekends. Essentially a job, I collected the prize money and they kept the ribbons. The couple lived in rooms inside their stable, across from the stalls. The arrangement taught me that enthusiasms run the gamut.

The husband showed "Fats" in parade classes, complete with silver-studded black saddle, breastplate, and bridle. Resembling Roy Roger's horse, Trigger, Fats was a handsome Tennessee Walker. His registered name was "Satan's Sunday Sun," appropriately, as he was bad-tempered until mounted, when he performed like a "push-button horse." Still, I was nervous and it shows in photographs. Judges prefer their contestants at ease and smiling. To think I could have earned more, simply by grinning. *Mmmm.*

The years passed and I found myself in northeast Wyoming. A friend's father owned a light gray thoroughbred mare named Sister, and he offered to sell her to me. She was "off the track," having raced a couple of years. *Mostly* calm, I knew she would need retraining. Tragically, she came to a bad end and had to be put down after spooking and running through our cattleguard one morning. It was horrendous. Our children were young and their lessons in death and dying began too soon. I recount that bitter morning in my book, *A Singular Notion*, and fictionalized this and another, happier cattleguard incident in my first novel, *The Riven Country of Senga Munro*.

The children's former babysitter in Douglas hauled up her needing-a-new-home quarter horse. A mare she was, and as such, could show some attitude. Chief among her penchants were nipping and the occasional kick, but once mounted (like Fats), she would calm. I accompanied my mother on a ride around our place, with her on Money Penny (renamed "Babe"), and me on True, whose story follows.

The seller insisted we take both the gray (True) and the sorrel yearling. "For the price of one!" he cajoled, two thoroughbreds. I was thrilled to my core. We named the yearling Roman. True was a sixteen-hand beauty, and his canter smooth as silk. Both horses had wonderful dispositions. I set about gentling the yearling and eventually saddled and trained him, a deed of which I'm inordinately proud. He did buck off our son once, and I take the blame, not having adequately prepared my boy, despite having joined some neighbors earlier in the summer for a two-day cattle drive, with me on True and John on a gentle horse. It was one of those iconic experiences—for those whose lives don't center on cattle ranching. "Our *Ranch Lite* experiences," the occasional gathers could be called, tongue in cheek. *Thanks, Rhoda and J.O.*

John did not "get back on the horse" immediately after being tossed, the age-old antidote, and a trip to the clinic confirmed a broken wrist. Since that day, I believe he's ridden only once, on an elk hunt with friends. I could be mistaken, but I doubt it. Piloting a small jet through turbulence may count.

Roman went to an area rancher who wanted to train him for team roping. He nicknamed him "Speedy." Well, I suppose he was, but before taking leave of us, and being still in possession of his capacities, he and Babe the mare became friendly. Thus, in May we enjoyed a blessèd event on the croft—the birth of a foal, coinciding with a visit from Jeff's father. Broad smiles ruled the day. It was that special.

We named the foal "Moon," as in "dark of the moon." A brown, not another bay, and after he was weaned, we sought another home for Babe. When it was time, I hired a trainer in Gillette to start Moon and, after a month, he returned home with the basic rudiments. As well, he'd load in our two-horse trailer, a handy skill. Sadly, Moon suffered an all-too-common malady, twisted gut, normally caused by colic. Our vet couldn't turn it, though he tried valiantly.

Doc recommended the horse doctor in Sturgis. We managed to load Moon, who was in pain, and I made the trip alone, my senses reeling with empathy and dread. Jeff had his job to attend to, and the kids, their schooling. My parents happened to be visiting from Georgia, fulfilling our yearly arrangement: one year they'd come to visit with us, the following, we'd travel to stay with them. Their comforting presence lent me strength, as only loved-ones can.

The vet confessed nothing could be done outside of an expensive surgery, which we weren't prepared to handle financially. He was a brave little steed, our Moon, as I sat at his face and neck, stroking him, while the vet tech administered the lethal dose.

I wept most of the long way home, not an optimal state at the wheel. I wept for Moon, surely, for his lost promise, for his sweetness and beauty, mostly for his friendship, but as the deaths of beloved pets often reveal, our grieving allows us to mourn those unconscious losses, those we tamp down, ignore or bury beneath a brave persona and sensibility. The loss of a pet often manifests as the proverbial straw that breaks the camel's back. Oh yes. And we indeed break. Into a million pieces.

If the misfortune happens to you (and sadly, it likely will if you keep pets), allow for time and privacy, and accept comfort. Accept the heartbreak, either in yourself or another, lest in the future unshed tears freeze hard into an icy heart. Conversely, permitted to flow, watery tears may transmute into their gaseous state as steam, to finally dissipate (it is to be hoped) in the touchless alchemy of grief.

For thirteen years, True graced the place, though I was seldom able to ride as much as his breed demands (two-plus hours a day, recommends one source). Thoroughbreds require much exercise. Their blood must be oxygenated regularly, on account of "higher maximum oxygen uptake" than other horses. It's true. You could look it up.

Over the years his gun metal coat lightened to bright clouds. When the cowboy arrived to take him away, the look in True's eyes was incredulous—and the wild gleam from my French drawing came alive. I hadn't prepared my friend and felt I had betrayed him. He was *true;* I was not. I wished him well and hoped for his good care.

The stable once dubbed "Fort Courage" by my father-in-law remained woefully vacant for two years. We had long ago sold off the flock of sheep and stopped raising chickens, turkeys, and guinea fowl, experiments to engage and foster our children's sense of responsibility. Ours too, truth be told. A skunk or two claimed the space under the tack room and feral cats slinked in and out, together with any number of mice or packrats (so not entirely abandoned). I grew lonesome just glancing down to the paddock and nursed a leaking heart—the kids' absence, to university, to their lives, and to their loves. Natural, if difficult, consequences of parenting.

One day Jeff came home from work with news. A colleague in Sundance knew a doctor in Lusk who wanted to find homes for several of his Arabians, as he was growing older and needed to cull his herd. Would we be interested? My heartstrings reached back to the sweet horse named Blue I showed when I was young and I beamed at Jeff. We made arrangements over the telephone and drove down one weekend, the horse trailer in tow. Dr. Huitt suggested I choose a fifteen-year-old mare named Zaraba, Z for short, as I'd requested a gentle horse. Another bay, she had the wide forehead characteristic of the breed. Her tail had once been broken, so it wouldn't flag as it should. I could not have cared less.

Jeff liked her immediately—a good sign. We rebuilt the paddock and she seemed to find her digs acceptable. Dr. Huitt drove up a few weeks later to check on her and, finding all well, he smiled and told me he was happy for Z. The good doctor passed away several years ago. He was a kind and generous soul.

Of particular joy, later, was lifting our one-year-old grandson onto the saddle for a ride and a photograph on his birthday. Wearing the cowboy hat our daughter had given him, Parker's image never fails to bring a smile. He was that loving. *Is* that loving.

Z lived fifteen more years, the last few "out to pasture," meaning, not ridden. We discovered in her papers that she was older than first believed, making her thirty-eight when she collapsed one day, and my husband did what no man wants to do. She lies buried beneath the oak tree beside Sister, Ned, Blackie, Cessna and Izzie. Rest ye well, friends.

Four years have passed. The stable yard again stands bereft of horse spirit. Z's heart may have failed, but I believe it was enlarged. She was that loving.

L *a Musica*

"Where words fail, music speaks," Hans Christian Andersen believed. A teacher once commented I never opened my mouth except to sing. This tendency, alas, is no longer the case. Ask my husband. I continue to play (on occasion) for weddings, funerals, birthday parties, and the odd festival or performance. When asked. In the end, the solace of music played, sung, or listened to, overcomes my ennui. Not boredom per se (I dislike the word—for insulting imagination), but ennui as world-weariness. Music soothes. I work up my tunes and the muse hears it. Not a Smaug-like dragon. More a yawning Brunhilda, complete with horned helmet. I jest.

Like a tap root, this deep connection grounds me to purpose and play. My heart skips a beat with the certainty that *Equus,* capitalized, has animated the *musical* ride on my rooting journey down, to tap a deeper aquifer for further inspiration. "Throw your heart over and the rest will follow," suggests the riding instructor to her students learning to jump. Universally applicable.

Faye Hipsher, as she was then known, offered me guitar lessons. As mentioned, she lived in the next block. *The Joan Baez Songbook* served as my primer. I've had to replace the copy for wearing it out. Faye would tirelessly jot down other lyrics and chords, and play the tune a few times until I had it. Like my father, I had a good ear, but I thank Mom for the voice.

Faye sang with a high, light, lilting voice and played her Gibson acoustic guitar with soft, clear precision. She later moved to Helen, in north Georgia, and became involved with Unicoi State Park's cultural programming. Faye passed in 1999, a year before Mom.

I spent long hours gingerly lifting a needle off a record so I could scribble down lyrics, practicing in our Georgia living room, away from the fray of a hectic household. Leaning against my headboard, cradling my guitar, I repeated verses of a song over and over to learn by heart, my fingertips burning from chording. Sickening stage fright only abated when I began taking blood pressure medication after a diagnosis. Oh, the lengths we'll go to in pleasing a demanding muse. She was bored with the same old repertoire.

At forty-something I took up the violin to read music more properly and to learn new tunes. On deeper analysis, I uncover a simpler fact: I love the sound. Like wind over a prairie.

Stored away, my record albums stand upright in their box to avoid warp. They include many of my parents' collection: 1,001 Strings; Piaf; an Andy Griffith comedy album among the lot. The cover art is a trip down memory lane. I recently downloaded Judy Collins' gorgeous 1970 album, *Whales and Nightingales,* from iTunes. Beloved music at our fingertips! Lyrics so easily available online! Brave New World, indeed, to have such [delights] in it. *Would Shakespeare have survived in this realm?*

Once upon a time I had a relationship with this particular album—and by extension, Miss Collins, *une chanteuse extraordinaire.* Listening to songs I steeped myself in during a personally difficult time, I sense neural pathways blaze with recognition. And their response? I tear up. From an underground spring of quiet joy. The former British slaver's hymn, "Amazing Grace," *happens* to be on the album. *Of course.*

Horseback riding, playing music, and singing all demand mindfulness. The word has entered our collective consciousness, itself a product of mindfulness. While here I limit focus to three experiences, the practice of attending to one's thoughts and feelings may (it is to be hoped) suffuse our consciousness, thereby leading to the storied "evolutionary leap," humanity may, or may not, attain. Awakened sensibilities remain dependent on compassionate behaviors—toward ourselves, and others.

When I began sitting zazen in the late Eighties, my perplexed mother asked me, "Why don't you just make riding your meditation time?" Did she practice a form of meditation when she cooked? When she lay on the couch in the den while my father talked back to the television? When she did the laundry, helped a woman in labor, or made a bed? I suspect she did; *praying ceaselessly* would have been a lesson imparted in nursing school by the Sisters of Charity. I wager Momma was a natural mystic, but her mind was her own.

Riding, on the other hand, spreads mindfulness throughout the body with capillaries, nerves, and arteries lighting up in a coordinated muscle memory between horse and rider. The same principle applies to playing an instrument, using the voice, or, yes, in writing. Now you see how this quality could apply to everything you do. A habitual musicality of movement and neurons.

Metaphorical taproots continue to push through, searching for optimum nourishment (or a desired effect)—justifying respect for the soil and its *terroir,* from the French: "The complete natural environment in which a particular wine is produced, including factors such as the soil, topography, and climate." By turns, the

"*goût de terroir*" refers to the characteristic taste of an environment—according to the New Oxford American Dictionary.

The upshot is Presence. Being present to ourselves is a capacity, dare I say, *a gift,* to be then passed on to others. The horses and music have been my teachers. What is more present than horses cavorting in a field, or lyrics flung into the air?

Figure 19 Graphite and Pencil Drawing of Horse, by Émile Lasalle

Figure 20 First Performance at U. of Wyoming Poke's Skeller, '71. Photo courtesy of 1972 WYO Yearbook

WINTER

*A*hh, Harvest Home. The happy phrase swings invisibly from an absent pole in our yard this time of year. In late fall as we scurry about, trying to cover late-ripening tomatoes, or, when picking out the grape vines or harvesting the apples, I occasionally toss the anticipation of a completed harvest before me, like a golden bocce ball. *Rest! I need rest! Or a beach vacation! Or a cruise up the River Seine!* The fantasies are indulged only as such before the chores are completed, as they would frustrate as untimely temptation.

By the calendar, winter begins on December 21, the Solstice, but we gauge the season by a more natural, traditional metric: the harvest is in and the apples have been pressed; the game has been processed and frozen; underground root crops have been dug (potatoes, carrots, *Echinacea* root, etcetera.) Reviewing my references to winter in earlier chapters, I recognize how the season has earned a separate status, apart from spring, summer, and fall. For growers, it is a welcome chance to lie fallow. The blessèd pause. This may arise from a future wish fulfillment—the gathering of provisions against the prospect of four or five cold months, the local grocery store notwithstanding. We have been *somewhat* industrious squirrels.

Winter is also the time for:

- Cleaning and sharpening tools.
- Pheasant hunting with man's best friend. *Outside of a book, a dog is man's best friend. Inside of a dog, it's too dark to read.* Thanks, Groucho, possibly by way of Oscar Wilde, only because it sounds *Wilde*-ish. . . .
- Watching more football games on television.
- Making sure the tractor battery is plugged in and charging, for plowing the road after heavy snowfall.
- Culling items from closets, drawers, pantry, bookcases, files, etcetera. A good resource is *Swedish Death Cleaning,* by Margareta Magnusson, *How to Free Yourself and Your Family from a Lifetime of Clutter.* The premise—you do not want to leave to your surviving spouse or family an onerous chore . . . . (or maybe you do . . . .)
- Taking up good books for long stretches of peaceful reading, cup of tea at hand, scented candle burning, woodstove crackling and quiet music in the background, preferably instrumental.

- Hanging and refilling bird feeders as needed. Jeff monitors several in the front yard and I tend one visible from my kitchen sink window. Chickadees, juncos, jays and American goldfinches are the most frequent winter visitors.

Earlier in these pages (in a footnote—spectacularly understated) I mention Jeff's fourth back surgery, but few circumstances. The agonizing pain began one year in early August. By October he required and underwent surgery. In early January, full wintertime, the pain had inexplicably returned, and the surgeon ordered another MRI. A cortisone shot administered in his spine eventually eased the pain. Longtime friend Tom Cowell arrived from Casper to help for a couple days with chores, i.e., emptying garbage bins, restocking the indoor wood store, and being generally pithy, supportive and encouraging. No pity-party allowed.

In the middle of this crisis, we made our sad goodbyes to our seventeen-year-old Jack Russell terrier, Eddy. A more heart-wrenching day hadn't come in a long while. What's more, the occupant of the White House was being impeached, the hearings ill-suited to healing, yet we were compelled to watch, witness, and whine.

If either of us is ever incapacitated—for one reason or another—you may well and correctly imagine the strain on the other. We aren't as young and foolish as we used to be (some might raise eyebrows at the second assertion), but if necessity is the mother of invention, then hiring help is the wise choice and solution. A call to the local school for a referral or recommendation has garnered at least two good hands, while the Amish colony will respond in fall, if anyone wishes "you pick" apples or grapes at a discount. A friend's housekeeper agreed to help me, if only monthly (on hiatus during the pandemic.) Word of mouth is still a most effective advertisement.

I include the above anecdotes to illustrate how circumstances may color perception of any experience. To wit, it might be best—and wise—to avoid all morbid thoughts. If one crops up, notice it, yes, then watch it float by, like an oak leaf in a stream.

Winter is famous for suggesting gloomy grim reapers, and a heaviness of heart did accompany our days with the marked absence of our indomitable terrier punctuating bleak forecasts. During any other year we would have simply recognized and accepted the habit of the season and carried on. Reading *The Winter of our Discontent* might have proven a remedy, in that paradoxical way the blues can alleviate misery. The classics are a powerful way to improve and enlighten your mind in the dark season. Steinbeck's title (borrowed from Shakespeare's *Richard III*) decries base corruption of a man's integrity, and might best be reserved for another year.

In winter our thoughts and fancies turn to travel. During the pandemic, they have taken on a more wishful-thinking aspect. *Fantasy Island*—if you like. I will review (just in case) the basic logistics of leaving our rabbit-warren home during the coldest season:

We turn off the water (hoses are drained at first freeze). House plants require a weekly/bi-weekly watering and buckets of rainwater may be stored in the studio/atrium for the purpose. You will notice an overlap with spring tasks here, the earlier weeks of the season feeling wintry in most respects.

Enlist, beg, or cajole a good neighbor to stop by, to confirm electricity and heat are in working order, and to please water the plants. I mull reducing indoor greenery, but after so long, several are counted as more than guests: "Martha," a grape ivy given to us by the mother of a dear friend gone too soon; the hoya, a redolent gift from Shirley; the jade, started from Lynn's plant and brought from Douglas, Wyoming, our previous residence; shamrock plants, a gift after my heart surgery—gifts of well-being, best wishes, and greening love.

I have observed travelers transporting their beloved plant friends on RV excursions. They enjoy the luxury of spaciousness—as opposed to a sedan or truck. I suspect our plant people are happy to see the backside of us at least once a year.

We enjoy Baja, Mexico and stay a week or two on the Pacific side, where we encounter winter-weary Americans and Canadians, friendly Mexican hosts, and humpback whales plying the waves with their calves. Sunshine, flowers, and the vast ocean greet us like goddesses opening wide their ample arms. I subscribe to this notion: *locality* filters one's thoughts and sensibilities, and the writing is infused with its flavor, apart from circumstances. My habit is to work in the mornings (feeling Hemingway-*ish*), and after, join Jeff for lunch and relaxation. I find him by the pool, chatting up other guests. Since the continental shelf drops precipitously from the stretch of beach, no swimming or wading is permitted because of riptide. Rogue waves increase the danger. Sitting or lying or meditating and gazing above *la orilla,* or shore, is permitted.

Our Mexican getaway has been suspended of late, as well as travel to Europe, Canada, and to family in far-flung states, for reasons mentioned. The cabin on Casper

Mountain, four hours south, is accessible only by skis or snowshoes. We miss its winter charms. In *A Singular Notion,* I describe the year Jeff and I lived in the "dry" cabin, melting snow on the wood stove in winter for water. We skied to and from our mountain jobs. By today's standards, the cabin would be called a "tiny house," designed to foster communication and cooperation, if guaranteeing moderate cabin fever. As antidote, we passed the muddy season of April 1977 train-hopping around Europe. It was an exceptional year. An adventure! A lark before settling down with children and weightier obligations. I highly recommend it.

In normal times (such a sad and facetious admission), the prospect of travel fuels our imagination and lends cheer. Travel magazines such as *Condé Nast* revel in dangling carrots of mouth-watering views (emphasis on water, the crucial element). Being a resident of a land-locked state, however beautiful, I crave an ocean view. It is a needful thing, and a matter of *perspective,* in terms of scope and scale. My place in the universe, and the utter improbability of humanity as a species, occurs to me as I sit on a sandy towel, crashing waves timed perfectly to my slowing breath. From Baja, I stare southward, tracing the 110° longitude, with *nada* between me and Antarctica but water.

By a similar sense of awe and humbling awareness, I consider snow-capped, rough peaks. We hold these dear in Wyoming. Contrast the action of gazing upon a vast, flat, sparkling ocean with that of wildly bucking uplifts of the Earth. In too obvious an analogy, swells of gigantic waves plough the sea *and* landscape—*my apologies.* For the time being, I contentedly settle for a river, lake, or pond in the Black Hills. The art of gentle compromise. In winter, if the gravel county road has been plowed, nearby Cook Lake restores the soul. We are all of us in need of restoration.

The word *restaurant* begs its restorative root, and I was recently reminded of this lovely linkage. Personally, I like to eat out on occasion. My husband is not so enamored, as he suffers from a dietary issue or two. Not to say he never joins me, as he will, but it's not his favorite activity. I, on the other hand, find that a room, semi-full of diners, engaged in a pleasantly civilized activity, balances my often-solitary habit. Patronizing area eateries substitutes for travel, if you count the varieties of cuisine available in a ninety-mile radius: Cajun, Mexican, Spanish, Italian, American, Chinese,

Japanese, German, Thai, Seafood, Indian, among others. A world of choice, and none requiring a passport. Unfortunately, dining indoors is ill-advised during the Covid-19 health crisis, but careful outdoor seating offers a semblance of culinary and societal pleasure.

In the meantime, we deliberate travel to Mexico and dream of a river cruise through Europe, only after completing long-postponed reunions with family and friends. Flying in the stone-cold face of an incipient wintry melancholy, we indulge and insist in making our plans, howsoever wryly the gods may laugh.

Figure 21 Sunset Sail with Jeff in Baja 2013

"May Their Memory Be a Blessing"

The newscaster closes his evening broadcast with the words after the network updates its Covid-19 report of the dead. I have hesitated to include the ongoing pandemic, but am at last nudged to, as witness, as mourner, as honest narrator. Just this morning I received a phone call from one of my sisters. A cousin (a favorite one, as it happens) died from the virus yesterday. He was only fifty-seven years old, and another of the family genealogists.

The year 2020 will likely be remembered as an *annus horribilis,* a terrible year, as the world awaited vaccination. Never in my nearly seven decades have I felt such dread for our country and the world. Not during the "Duck and Cover" scare of the Fifties and early Sixties. Not during later anti-war protests, riots, and assassinations and not during more recent terrorist attacks—foreign and domestic. I have lived as a child, in relative terms, blithely pursuing the American dream of happiness and fulfilment. My opinion has necessarily evolved around those contexts.

As a post-World War II baby, I benefited from an incredible era of progressive expansion and opportunity, while my father served the country in three hot wars and, later, during the Cold War. He shouldered massive burdens of responsibility and overwhelming cares. Somehow, the weight of mentally preparing for all-out war while waging peace seeped through his beautiful sensibilities. It was like a threatened dam against pressure cracks. Our family, and in a much larger sense the entire country, absorbed a cognitively dissonant energy via osmosis. Nations succumbed to a kind of species-wide schizophrenia. It permeates the fragile psychology of the world's peoples—unto even the physical planet, if I may say. The scientists tell us we have until 2030 to reverse a desperate climate change catastrophe. Earth will survive. *Humanity?*

Nations have endured and withstood constant vibrational malaise, vis-à-vis opposing forces, since it became apparent the human race could destroy itself. Mutually Assured Destruction is the glib reminder. My father compartmentalized his horrific concerns from our family, but "we are all connected," as they say, and on a cellular level we all contracted it—Mom, my siblings and me. We simply knew what he knew, but more disturbingly, he understood the particulars while we absorbed, if unconsciously, the raw emotion. As I alluded to earlier, the crushing burden finally took its toll—even unto the present. The twentieth century *was* a violent one, and the twenty-first reaps the whirlwind, a frightful twister of greed, hatred and delusion; heartbreak, misery, and pain. . . .

I revisit Thomas Jefferson's brief "Bible" from time to time, the one he edited by separating "diamonds from dunghill" (his term) from the Gospels. He named his effort *The Philosophy of Jesus of Nazareth*. The teachings are emphasized, those Jefferson believed rang true, and in writing to Charles Thompson in 1816, he admitted: "A more beautiful or precious morsel of ethics I have never seen; it is a document in proof that I am a *real Christian,* that is to say, a disciple of the doctrines of Jesus. . . ."

Our third president evidently had little patience for clerics and their like. Separation of Church and State, as we all know, was only one of his rallying cries, but a forceful one. And my point? Reminded of one salient observation by the teacher, to reap what we sow is a karmic principle. *What goes 'round comes 'round.* Physics may attest, and, lest we forget, we *do* reap what we have sown in life, the principle aptly drawn by the Nazarene, whom I daresay was crucified solely because he and the Jewish power structure disagreed. In planting his new seeds, Jesus not only "raised the consciousness" of his listeners (the phrase grows dull with ambivalence), he lifted high a burning torch, so his followers could better see themselves in one another. That he died "for our sins" is often quoted, but I disagree, respectfully. I believe he was sentenced to death for much the same reason as Socrates was condemned four hundred years earlier, *officially,* for "corrupting" the populace—if not the impressionable youth of Athens. And yet, and yet, I am enthralled by him.

The world is awash and drowning in consequences, and as well, from more frequent and powerful winds. It is as though she is desperately trying to throw off some ragged interloper. Or, conversely, she burns, as Australia and South America have seen, felt, smelled, tasted, and heard. The western United States and Canada's west coast skies reflect orange and red from the flames. The sun can scarcely wink—a baleful crimson eye behind the smoke, grit, and ash.

It is high time to sow new seeds, and may I state the obvious by dent of simple observation—we might begin by seeking practical means to evaluate, appraise, and consider much more carefully our decisions—and, our common aspirations. The Native American's traditional entreaty, *to be accountable to seven generations forward,* serves here. Our choices today are myriad and could be infinitely better curated. Decisions *are* the seeds we sow, hence the ardent plea for discernment. Honest effort is crucial. Perfect mindfulness is relegated to the sleep of death. Memory as blessing is a worthy intent—and seed—but our inner soil must first be tended and fertilized with more love. *More love.* Rest in peace, cousin.

WINTER II

The 2020 Presidential Election is history. November 3, 2020 saw a bumpy night, to invoke Betty Davis. Whatever transpires, our work has only just begun, never mind the occupant of the White House. Vaccines against Covid-19 are developed and being administered, while the number of dead has exceeded the tragic count for our country's World War II fatalities. The wearing of masks and physical distancing is summarily ignored by many, as are appeals to vaccinate. This and the previous chapter read as an appeal.

Why ever would I include a mention of politics in this, a homestead manual and *radical* memoir? Our roots resolutely interlace and cling to a most magnificent idea so many have given their lives to defend. That of self-governance. Once and forever endowed (such an elegant word) with what Thomas Jefferson first deemed a *sacred* right, Benjamin Franklin substituted "self-evident" for the religious term, with Jefferson's blessing—in order to appease a pragmatic, secular bent in the population. "Life, Liberty and The Pursuit of Happiness" unquestionably remains an ideal, initially denied to American Indians and the enslaved peoples from the African continent. However, *realizing* a "more perfect Union" is the ongoing work of conscience, a matter of the will and a motive for a striving necessity of action. The time for excuses is over.

"Our new Constitution is now established, and has an appearance that promises permanency; but in this world nothing can be said to be certain, except death

and taxes." Franklin expressed the caveat in a letter to Jean-Baptiste Le Roy in 1789, borrowing the salient phrase from Daniel Defoe in *The Political History of the Devil,* written in 1726. It must have made an impression. The pairing of death and taxes is earlier made in *The Cobbler of Preston,* written in 1716 by Christopher Bullock. I raise the provenance to: 1. make light of a glib statement; 2. address a current hypothesis; and 3. to review a somewhat tedious winter activity.

But first, in blatant procrastination, let's check the trap lines.

Several chores cross seasonal boundaries— monitoring mouse traps in the storeroom and atrium area, for instance. Consider it an occupational hazard of living in the country. Below the house, the lonesome stable shelters the occasional, itinerant mouse catcher. Neither dear husband nor Gabe the yellow Lab would abide a cat in the house, or the stable, as it happens. Recently, a ginger cat and our dog attacked one another, and Gabe suffered a bite before chasing said cat up a pole. This landed our defender at the veterinary clinic overnight for antibiotics, an I.V. and anti-inflammatories. It seems the bite from a cat can lead to sepsis if not treated. Jeff set a live trap in the barn, redolent with sardines.

Reveling in the hunt, Gabe presents us freshly killed voles that overrun the flower/herb gardens. The wee beasts create tunnels and raid the sleeping iris bulbs for winter provisions. We planted solar-powered, high-pitch repellents. These actually deter them. The next best thing would be to clear out much of the brush in front of the house. My so-called "cottage garden" dies back yearly from a wild collection of mints, Bouncing Bets, Veronica plants, irises, and catnip. It is *all* catnip to the rodents.

The cat was trapped and has been removed from the premises. I omit the air quotes. Another feral feline will likely take his place in the stable.

On to taxes, another business of politics. Before we hired an accountant, Jeff prepared the documents. I am constitutionally ill-suited for any such endeavor. What I can do (and do do), is to keep adequate track of receipts, etc., related to deductions (when those must be summarized). And no, our tax man does not resemble the grim reaper in any way. Death and taxes have been *conflated,* an overused word today. As citizens, I believe taxes and voting are opposite sides of the same "coin of the realm."

Public opinion careens out of control, sharpened by fear, bitterness and deep disappointment. "A lack of moral commitment" is how friend Ann frames the impasse (at my gentle prod, the obvious having escaped me). The country is in crisis, constitutionally or no. Collectively, I believe we are experiencing what Jungian psychologists dub our *shadow,* that what we ignore or do not accept in ourselves, mostly unconsciously, we project onto the other. Integrating one's shadow is vital work; all the more so for an entire country.

South Africa, recall, only began to heal following Apartheid after the Truth and Reconciliation project was initiated. In the U.S. the metric has been used to bring rapists and their victims to forgiveness and acceptance— never dismissal or a forgetting of the violation. By speaking truthfully and listening to one another, by owning their behavior and sharing how the rape impacted their lives, they are released from a stranglehold and are able to go forward with their lives, despite a sentence to serve for one, and post-traumatic stress syndrome for another—a sentence to serve, nevertheless.

A paradigm shift occurs when we are in possession of new information. Our thinking and sensibilities must necessarily adjust. Essentially, we are in the midst of such a shift, what Patricia Sun, the aforementioned Philosopher of Wholeness, has called, "an evolutionary leap." Some might quip we are experiencing *a devolution.* The possible human is yet to evolve. *Will there be time?* But evolution is a process, not a destination. Or is it? And anyway, how much more perfect could a peach taste? A *more* perfect Union rests on organic principle. No judgment call. Ever *becoming.* Even in death.

When divisions and polarizations stretch so far afield, as now, I envision a textbook electron microscope image of mitosis, when the cell finally splits in half. As a nation—as *nations,* on the macro level, this is scary stuff. At present we stand in anaphase, where the chromatids of chromosomes have separated and stretch, like fingers, toward their poles, hence, "polarized." *We the People* becomes Us against Them. Not conducive to a viable union, though the Founders wisely gave us a working model for dealing with impasse and disagreement. To arrive at something approaching compromise *and* wise governance is damned hard work. It demands qualified captains at the helm.

How are roots germane to the above? Certain plants must become root-bound in their container before they can bloom. Our Hoya, for example. (*Bear with me a moment.*) It may be our country has become root-bound after 245 years, less if you count the Civil War as an instance when those roots were disturbed. And it may be, as a result, we shall one day bloom in unexpected ways. As we have before. The Hoya surprises us first by releasing the sweetest fragrance at dawn and at dusk. The flowers are singular gifts of beauty. May we glimpse the *possibility* of healing in our land before the reality. I must believe it.

My father and I shared a love of science fiction, and my son inherited the interest. In one more white-rabbit chase, I propose—with others—the genre acts as oracle, similar to Delphi of yore, poets and sci-fi authors as prophets and seers: Bradbury, Asimov, L'Engle, Heinlein, Clarke, Le Guin, and N.K. Jemisin, to name a few. Personal favorites include Marion Zimmer Bradley, Mary Oliver, and Shakespeare (yes, in one breath!). Film adaptations may reimagine tales, and they occasionally succeed.

Near the end of the first *Planet of the Apes,* Charlton Heston's character falls to his knees after discovering the verdigris diademed head of the Statue of Liberty (the rest of the monument buried in sand). With shocked realization, the astronaut understands he has been on Earth all along. Decrying earlier inhabitants who squandered a rare gift, he damns them with a desperation born of despair.

May we not look back on this time and curse, lest we be the very ones we are damning. Take care of one another and your holy homestead, however humble or grand. Take care of Wyoming. Moreover, take precious care of this country and all Lady Liberty represents. She also stands atop the U.S. Capitol as "Freedom." Her improbable appearance on our shores was by design, my hypothesis, not by accident.

Once, as part of a writing workshop, I completed a survey to ascertain my core values. It seems their identification is desirable if you would convey truths and fancies. Unsurprising to me, on every level, was discovering I value Freedom above all. As an umbrella value, it covers about everything. Patricia Sun (also) says we retain our liberty by *living* it, moment to moment, by carefully considering hidden consequences and choosing well. I often fail, but this notion shines brightly as ideal. A torch lifted high.

Figure 22 Looking south

The quiet stillness of winter invites notions, philosophies, and fancies. Walks wait until after lunch, when the temperature reaches the optimal degree for the day. Longer phone conversations or digital talks with friends and family fill in afternoons and weekends. Stories need telling, either on the page or breathed as a tune into the air. The usual mundane housekeeping chores beckon, and the occasional guest drops by. During the pandemic we sit outdoors. We look forward to proper visits, principally with our children and grandchildren.

If and when a radical change of priorities appears in our future, I pray for the strength and courage to meet it. I dangle "if," suspecting I whistle Dixie—old times there not forgotten.

Born and raised in rural Alabama as a "red dirt" girl, my mother picked a lot of that "land of cotton." She once told me how her finger tips ached and burned afterward, the bolls prickly and razor sharp. The family move to Charleston, South Carolina, must have felt like the Exodus.

I live in awe of ancestors, whose DNA trickles down through our being. I have picked cotton through my mother, flown a P-47 in wartime through my father, doctored in early Louisiana and, in some distant past, called myself "Norman," after the Scandinavians who colonized northern France in the tenth century.

We belong to countless unknown relatives—the fact made all the more poignant *by* the not-knowing. These roots and radical beginnings twine even now through our children's lives. Organic spirals of mitochondria, and eventual stories, thread their way into our lives. Unseen alliances reach back to the stars, to inform our sensibilities, hopes, and destinies.

It is not lost on me that I am mining ore and am, in turn, excavated by literary characters and events. Through writing, I integrate the sheer magic of consciousness with an overarching desire for expression. In the world of Franklin's, where "nothing can be said to be certain," there exists a common and saving purpose. It *shall* present itself sooner or later. And if the purest and simplest purpose is to live well, then—as Wyoming author Gaydell Collier once quipped to then aspiring novelist W. Michael Gear, "*Dontcha think you'd best be about it?*" Hers is the mantra agitating my thoughts like a ringer-washer these days, accompanied by the late Justice Ruth Bader Ginsberg's wise counsel (especially during a long quarantine with one's spouse): "In every good marriage, it helps sometimes to be a little deaf."

BEAU SOLEIL

arth-anchored" to a south-facing slope above the orchard, the new array of solar voltaic panels stands like a slightly tilted collection of Space Odyssey monoliths and we grin in agreement, "It's *so cool!*" Just east of this thirty-eight-foot-long structure squats an eight-by-twelve greenhouse, all perky, bright and expectant. Automatic roof vents open to evacuate rising indoor temperatures. A hydraulic tube-like chamber, filled with liquid, expands when warm, to push a piston that opens a lever, which raises the window. An opposite sequence with chill. *Take note*—the mechanisms must be removed in winter against freezing.

Two of the three roof windows face south, putting me in mind of eyes, winked open, to entice the sun for another six weeks of growing season. The hopeful plan, anyway. Jeff has pined for a greenhouse for years, perhaps decades, while I have long considered the practicality of solar energy. I count as good omen the following astonishing sight as we discussed the matter with the electrician from Sheridan: We were sitting in the orchard (safely distancing ourselves during the pandemic), when Rick spoke up, *real* casual-like, "There's a herd of elk. . . ."

We have heard bugling twice (in three decades) and have spotted scat, but I've never seen the animals so close to our home. And here they were, just across the highway, about a hundred and fifty yards away, loping down from the canyon where we believe they reside. Something must have spooked them, as it was midday, their usual rest time. Bow hunters sprang to mind, or a mountain lion. In all their glory, a great antlered bull herded his harem of cow elk, a younger bull trailing behind him. It was exhilarating, to state the obvious. Odd too, as elk and white tail deer seldom share territory. I ran for my phone to take a photograph, but Rick was able to snap some as his cellphone was at hand. He shared them.

Figure 23 Elk Across Valley. Richard Mack Photo

I subconsciously subscribe to portents and the like. Encouragement and, equally, discouragement, demand support. We require the still, small voices in our heads and hearts. Some might snicker *"magical thinking,"* but if *Life*—that Conestoga (or is it more a humble sheepherder's wagon?)—isn't tied to a star of wishful thinking, I don't know what is. A phrase I hear all too often today says, "It is what it is." The Zen suggests ultimate reality, but I chafe at the utter bleakness behind it. The French quip, *c'est la vie*—that's life—with a philosophical pout and Gallic shrug answers for me. More in keeping with *Oh, well!* instead of Eeyore's "Let's all just lie down now and die. . . ." It all depends on tone, as so much does.

So! A new project or two eases the sad restrictions accompanying the pandemic, and even without it, the time had long passed to face the reality of a warming planet. As further incentive, the solar technician has all but promised our initial investment will be returned in ten to twelve years—beyond the window scientists have predicted for us to get our act together, vis-à-vis climate change. This window of opportunity is reportedly shrinking, however. A second incentive—we may also file for a twenty-six percent deduction on our taxes. (*I began to write "tongue in cheek," prefacing the prior statement, but find the sarcasm obscene, given the circumstances.*)

Contemplate incentive, given the dire predictions.

In the event back-up well water electricity is required, I'm disappointed to learn we would need to upgrade to a large battery package, but Rick reminds us of our gasoline generator. We had hoped for the cleaner alternative in an emergency. In any event, the energy produced by solar panels alone will offset much of what we do use, and the utility company will credit back the kilowatts produced in equal measure, according to a "net metering" agreement. At this writing, the Wyoming legislature is considering a bill disallowing an equal trade in the future. You bet I'm contacting committee members.

C'est la vie may be thwarted on occasion, depending on circumstances.

The sweet greenhouse provides a perfect habitat for earlier germinations, and sufficient time for the season's later-ripening tomatoes. Pulled up before a freeze, we hang the plants upside-down to finish. It's win-win, and not a zero-sum game. Life is not strictly a transactional affair, as some might insist. Reaping what we sow may sound vaguely like an exchange, but it isn't. Not exactly.

It may be better viewed as an agreement made with our soul.

The company who designed this greenhouse model are geniuses. *Grandio,* out of Idaho, is providing a service, and have lately sold hundreds of models. *In case the famine should happen,* I say in less snarky tone than quipped in the past. (Picture a Yiddish crone, that would be me—but not Yiddish.) It took two days to put the greenhouse together, with help. My husband calls instructions, "destructions." (A joke, but not entirely.) I haven't seen him so pleased in months.

The greenhouse offers another dimension to homesteading. That of choice. Upon its completion, we sit outdoors under garage eaves, to gaze lovingly at our new ~~baby~~ addition. I locate a rechargeable light bulb and hang it from one of the trusses. The polycarbonate walls and ceiling (Plexiglass-like, but stronger and double-paned) bend the light, flashing it around the entire perimeter in a bright, diffuse line. I remark that folks driving by might think an alien has landed in our back

yard. With the solar panels' appearance, it's for certain.

Rising from my seat, frosty Corona Light in hand, I wander over to the glowing object of our delight, now lighted from within and, pouring a small libation onto the interior space, I thank the powers that be for such wonderful things, this greenhouse and the array. After an ancient custom dating back some 5,000 years, it was believed the dead must eat dust, so the ritual of pouring out wine, or later, liquor, evolved as means to quench their thirst.

"May you never thirst," Robert Heinlein's blessing in *Stanger in a Strange Land* grows more and more fitting the older I grow. The elements and time conspire against me. The greenhouse is also "earth anchored." Let me explain, as ever so often it will prove necessary to tighten bolts, screws, etcetera. Placed evenly around the structure, the twelve-inch-long, single-helix steel spirals are buried in quick-setting concrete and attached to the underlying foundation. A "just-in-case" reference with pertinent information on the greenhouse and the solar array system may be of assistance. Just in case.

TO LIVE AMONG TREES

The West, including our county, is suffering a drought. Literally and figuratively, in my view. Fires threaten the west coast and, nearer, a massive burn in southeast Wyoming and Colorado destroyed thousands of acres. Summoning Aquarius, the Water Bearer, to Earth, I pray for three things: mercy, a quenched thirst for justice, and the possibility of peace.

Trees need water and the Earth needs trees. The native ponderosa pines deserve pride of place, much as Richard Powers has honored redwoods in his magnificent novel, *The Overstory*. To *simply* live among trees remains my fervent wish. The vanilla-scented bark of ponderosa seemingly drifts over the Black Hills, like an unhurried tide. Young saplings encroach upon empty "parks." We are astonished at the sudden appearance of new stands of pines, knowing it was not abrupt at all, but we had merely been occupied elsewhere, distracted, as the tree babies hurriedly established themselves while we weren't looking.

Two days ago, as I trudged up the road toward the house after collecting the mail, I stood arrested in my snowy tracks by the sound of roaring—the freight train variety, no beast. Normally ascribed to a warning of tornados, I quickly dismissed that possibility and detected the source: a gyrating wind swirled through a swaying stand of pines just north of the house. A whirlwind? The phenomenon was restricted to an area the size of a McMansion. The top third of the trees undulated for several moments like drunken sailors, and then the roar moved to the adjacent stand, disturbing (or exciting) those trees for approximately the same amount of time—the uncanny bit. The rhythmic animation continued into the crook of the ridgetop, and then all was silent once more.

Blessed, I was. By a wind at play in the fields of the Lord. *Thank you, Peter Matthiessen.*

In his comprehensive volume, *The Black Hills,* Col. Richard Irving Dodge, a member of the 1875 U.S. Army expedition, "equipped with scientific instruments," lyrically describes the environs:

> Grand mountains, frowning crags, gloomy abysses, dense forests and intricate jungles alternate with lovely parks, smooth lawns, and gentle slopes. Each portion of the Hills has its own especial peculiarities of scenery. The tops of the grand mesas are lovely with long grasses and flower-covered slopes, set as it were in frames of the dark green forests of pine. Lower down, the slopes become ravines, then cañons. . . .
>
> As we leave the upper surface in either direction, we find in this forest openings, larger or smaller, sometimes several miles in extent and very irregular in shape. The surface and soil are apparently identical with that covered with timber, yet there is not a tree or shrub, nothing but a rich green carpet of grass. This is a "Park." These lovely

openings add not a little to the beauty of
the scenery.[2]

That Colonel Dodge likens the Hills to Vermont is
lovely, if a mark of poetic license—as I have committed
myself, repeatedly, with no apologies. The Hills
comprise 8,424 square miles; Vermont, 9,623. One day,
I would love to judge his comparison for myself, having
occasionally fancied our landscape as being *elsewhere*—
aside from our friend's jubilant Tuscan reference. Our
childhood nanny, Micheline, and her daughter Paola
paid a visit in the late Eighties. Both declared the
country a lunar landscape. I took it to mean the isolation
reminded them of being on the moon. But travel to
Vermont and Tuscany would be welcome—a long road
trip with a leg gracefully swung over the ocean.

Mulling the next task, Jeff lists the repainting of apple
tree trunks. This prompted a review of basic botany as
we soaked away aches and ennui in the hot tub. Before
us stood the Dalgo crab apple tree, its weathered lower
trunk spotted with peeling white latex paint. When
visitors first see the painted bark, they invariably ask the
reason. In a nutshell, a warm snap in winter, say, in
February or March, may cause the sap (think *blood,* or
don't) to begin flowing too early, forcing blooms and
exposure when a later spring snow storm grips the area.
The longer explanation: xylem and phloem, you may
remember, are both saps, or "vascular tissues." Xylem
flows from the roots, bringing water, nutrients and
minerals from the roots, while phloem flows up and

---

[2] *The Black Hills,* by Richard Irving Dodge, Lieut.-Colonel, U.S.
Army; Ross & Haines, INC. Minneapolis, 1965; pages 48-49

down, transporting nutrients and food from leaves to other growing parts of the plants or, in this case, the tree.

No such unseasonable warming this week, however. The forecast warns of single digits, to reach a -10° high toward the weekend, with wind chill factors well below zero. It's *friggin'* cold, but the polar blast comes accompanied by snow, a good thing. Every centimeter helps ground moisture. The solar techie in Sheridan suggested we ignore the array's energy production in January and February, as we might be disappointed. Snow cover, cloud cover—each interfere with sunshine reaching the panels. Jeff does his best to sweep off the snow, but even with a long broom handle, the top half remains white for now. Snow slides off of its own accord eventually.

Figure 24 The Orchard after Spring Rain

White latex paint, white snow—both provide a cushion of insulation against the powerful force of our sun, the former by virtue of simple reflection; the latter, by paradox. (Think of living in an igloo.) I love to contemplate the orchard when the trees are newly painted and tended; snappy dressers all, each tree wears the arboretum version of spats. Waters of mercy, justice and peace can't be far behind. We'll all dress up for that day. Maybe even wear hats.

Figure 25 The Walk

RECIPES

The title of this and the following chapter share a root (*see what I did there?*). You might think it is *re*, but no; *recipe* derives from "receipt," whose origin has to do with *to take*. We "take" our remedies or medicines. See the *med* in the two latter words? So, a two-for-one. I enjoy word play, but resist crossword puzzles. Dad worked them with ball-point pen and was happy to inform us of this gift.

Mom continued to hone her cooking skills (though she wouldn't have considered it a "practice"). Attending classes at the Paris Cordon Bleu School of Cooking may have brought a measure of peace and purpose in the wake of tragedy. I have mentioned how she and other Air Force wives organized day trips into the City of Light. God knows she needed some brightness. She may have sought the worthier objective, apart from a mere Girls' Day Out. Mom was less comfortable in society than she might have confessed. She learned to play "act as if," *very* well.

Where are you going with this? you might wonder.

We all seek comfort in times of trouble; we might wish for the dignity of work, at the very least—a *measure* of energy transfer, as described in physics. We long for purpose—even if unconsciously, I believe. Cooking (notwithstanding the grand scale of French cuisine) is an art, and it often begins with the simplest ingredients and methods. Via Italy during the Renaissance, the needful art is rooted in the halls, marble or not, of humanity's history. At least this is how I picture *Cooking,* if I were creating a compendium of a mother's art.

When I was a junior in high school, Mom offered to cook a "real French meal" for our high school French Club. Extra leaves slipped into the dining room table, set with the good china, we managed to seat at least a dozen classmates. I felt self-conscious, taking my father's usual place, a regal Louis XIII arm chair. Jeff and I have since had the carved oak chair collection refurbished and reupholstered. I named four of them and their carved mustachioed faces after the Four Musketeers: *Porthos, Athos, Aramis* and *D'Artagnan.* The arm chair is of course saved for "Milady." But let's return to our feast, now that introductions have been made.

Boeuf Bourguignon was the main course, followed by a salad, French bread, and cheese. Alas, no wine— though it's entirely possible we were served a tiny amount, given my parents' sensibilities. I honestly don't remember. I mention the evening to illustrate my mother's generous nature. Cooking was her canvas and instrument. She was the willing participant of her life.

To be fair, I include several sources in this personal collection: a couple of Dad's recipes, via his friends— likely after a certain amount of imbibing (to test it!)—as in the case of William Wister Haines' Mint Juleps. The screenwriter's uncle was Owen Wister, author of *The Virginian.* Dad made Mr. Haines' acquaintance in 1952 Hollywood, when both were involved with filming the Korean War drama, *One Minute to Zero.*

The recipe for Texas Chili came from dear Dick Deardorff, with whom Dad hunted ducks on occasion. The notorious BBQ sauce has unknown provenance. My grandmother's desserts and my father-in-law's BBQ sauce round out the collection. More a sampling than a full menu.

Please consider, any amount of making a recipe your own is encouraged, if to a point. Interpretation is key in life. The caveat: know when to follow instruction, and how a change might affect the whole. I cite Picasso's oft-repeated rule: "Learn the rules like a pro, so you can break them like an artist." The use of sensible parameters, whether in poetry, cooking, or politics, guards against chaos. Another caveat any chess player knows: *do read through the entire recipe before you begin.* These are principles my momma never taught me, by the way. She held her art close and kept her own counsel. This may have proven a crucial ingredient in keeping her wits intact.

Some lessons, cooking or not, we learn the hard way. Was I merely inattentive, or obstinate? More likely the latter. I could have learned much by simple observation, but her eldest daughter was the consummate tomboy, you see, and Mom's broken-spined copy of *The Joy of Cooking* held not one iota of interest to me. It catches up with you, I'm here to say, a latent respect for this life-affirming, nurturing joy of life. Tara Brach, the Buddhist teacher whose podcast reflections ease my pandemic fears and isolation, suggests a revision to Darwin's "survival of the fittest" thesis, in promulgating Louis Cozzolino's phrase: "the survival of the nurtured."

Amen. Just as a soil's minerals, microbes, and water nourish the roots of mighty trees, a living culture of family favorites nurtures soul roots and ensures deep roots. Our birthright ties to Mother Earth are magnified and strengthened.

I hope you will try some of these delights. Mom once told me that if she used only one recipe in a cookbook, it was worth the price of the volume. I have retained the colloquial ease with which these recipes were jotted, in homage, and I duly apologize for any confusion.

One of her drip-stained go-to's was titled Charleston Receipts, *from which she made "Shrimp for Breakfast." The dish, paraphrased here, remains a family favorite and shall be first in our affections. I prefer the larger shrimp, as it is easier to avoid drowning in the water, affecting taste. This is wonderful with a salad and French bread.*

SHRIMP FOR BREAKFAST

> 1 1/2 cups medium to large peeled raw shrimp
> 2 tablespoons chopped onion
> 2 teaspoons green pepper
> Salt and pepper
> 1 teaspoon Worcestershire sauce
> 3 tablespoons bacon grease
> 1 teaspoon catsup
> 1 1/2 tablespoons flour
> 1 cup water or more

Fry onion and green pepper in bacon grease. When onion is golden, add shrimp; turn these several times with onion and pepper. Add enough water to make a sauce, about one cup. Do not cover shrimp with water or your sauce will be tasteless. Simmer 2 or 3 minutes and thicken with flour and a little water made into a paste. Add seasoning, Worcestershire sauce, and catsup. Cook slowly until sauce thickens. Serve over grits. Serves four.

In France, our housekeeper and sometime-cook, Julienne, may have been responsible for this version of the nourishing meal. It's a favorite. Returning home from school one day, I once found the sparrow-like woman stirring a huge pot of sugared currants to make jelly. It smelled wonderful. Léon, our neighbor's gardener, tended the row of currant bushes in the side yard. Imagine Julienne harvesting the tiny berries, and then making conserves for her employers. Obviously, much more figured in the relationship. Making jam is a labor of love.

Today I use the food mill, or sieve, *that Mom bought in Moret-sur-Loing at a shop in the late 1950s. The redoubtable owner recognized l'Américaine when Mom returned with two of my three French-born sisters, Felicia and Alexandria, four decades later. Mom came home with a shiny new stainless-steel version of her old food mill, along with several packages of Brie.*

The trick is mastering the texture of this soup. Which is why using a blender won't do. You do not want mush. The larger rice or pea-size holes work best when choosing the correct disc. Mom noted that one may use "fresh, frozen or canned vegetables" when making the soup. As sodium levels are a concern to many, if you're using canned, you might drain the contents and rinse them with water. As for soup bones, I like to use two or three beef short ribs, the meatier the better.

MILLIE LATIOLAIS' FRENCH VEGETABLE SOUP

Cook soup bones in ½ gallon of water with salt and pepper. After boil, simmer about ½ hour, then add: 2 pounds chopped potatoes, 6 medium onions, chopped; 2 #2 cans mixed vegetables (or fresh/frozen); 3 #2 cans of tomatoes, 1 can of green beans, 1 can of butter beans, 1 can of okra, 1 hot green chili pepper. Season with a bay leaf, parsley, a dash of red pepper. Simmer for 2 hours. Sieve in a food mill, scraping the bottom often into the pot.

With six children, and friends dropping in when they learned she was making her soup, Mom came to use her generous five-gallon copper pot after quadrupling the ingredients. She served it with parmesan cheese sprinkled on top, and the hearty cornbread listed below, made with sour cream and creamed corn. Needless to say, it was an all-day affair of the heart, this simple soup meal, and we justly praised it, and her. She did warn me repeatedly, "You know that's NOT a low-calorie dish," when I would fill my bowl again. And again.

Figure 26 Moret-sur-Loing, France

SOUR CREAM   CORNBREAD

You may marvel or cringe at Mom's frequent use of sour cream. There is a lesson in here somewhere, à propos savoring the sweet with the sour in life. We often enjoyed this cornbread. She was an Alabama girl, after all.

> 1 ½ cup corn meal
> 1 ½ cup flour
> ½ teaspoon salt
> 1 teaspoon baking powder
> 2 eggs
> 2/3 cup vegetable oil
> 1 cup of sour cream
> 1 #2 can creamed corn.

Mix well. After heating ¼ cup oil in a large skillet, add the batter and bake at 375° for 40 minutes.

Figure 27 Mom, Cooking

DICK DEARDORFF'S TEXAS CHILI

Dick and my father liked to visit in our small wood-paneled den in Marietta, endlessly talking back to television news programs between conversation points. Dick was a kind man and a friend, in my recollections. No one should ever have to discover a friend's body, but Dad did. After trying to reach his friend by phone one day, Dad finally drove over. I suspect he was dreading what he'd find. "No one dies who is remembered with love." And assisted by a good recipe.

3 pounds of boneless chuck, in 1" cubes.

2 tablespoons vegetable oil

2-3 garlic cloves, minced

4-6 tablespoons chili powder

2 tablespoons cumin

3 tablespoons flour

1 tablespoon oregano leaf

2 cups, 13 ¾ oz can beef broth

1 teaspoon salt

¼ teaspoon pepper

Optional: 1 can pinto or kidney beans, 1 cup sour cream, 1 lime, cut in wedges

Heat oil. Add beef. Lower heat, add garlic. Combine chili, cumin, flour, and oregano over meat. Add 1 ½ cans broth, stir. Add salt and pepper. Cool, put in fridge overnight. Reheat. Serve with sour cream, over rice, if desired. Serve with lime wedges.

Note the no-frills manner. All Dick.

JAMBALAYA

This is a "pinch of this, a pinch of that" recipe. Its ease is what makes it so welcome. Like most things Cajun, ease defines The Sweet Life. Another one of those obvious generalities, but in this

case, mostly true. A life-long resident of Louisiana, my grandmother on my father's side answered to "Mama Ease," short for "Louise."

Mix 2 teaspoons red pepper, 1 ½ teaspoons salt, pepper, thyme, rubbed sage, or use Cajun seasoning. Set aside. Brown meat in a stick of butter (chicken, ham, sausage, shrimp—this recipe lends itself to leftovers). Remove to roasting pan. In a skillet, brown 1 cup green pepper, 1 cup onion, 1 cup celery (the Holy Trinity of Cajun cooking), 2 tablespoons minced garlic (or more). Remove to roaster. Heat 4 ½ cups chicken broth, 1 cup chopped tomatoes, 1 can of tomato paste or 1 cup sauce, 2 bay leaves.

In roaster, sprinkle over meats 2 cups rice; over this pour broth mixture. Cover and roast for 1 hour at 350°. Stir once or twice carefully during baking period. Fix a fruit salad and serve with French bread.

FRENCH BREAD

I figured out this recipe when Jeff and I were living our "Walden Experiment" on Casper Mountain in Wyoming at his father's small cabin. I include the instructions in my 2006 memoir, A Singular Notion. *I still think of all cooking as "practical magic." Here are the original notes, revised:*

After a month-long Eurail trip through Europe with Jeff in the spring of 1977, I was determined to make French bread, even in our cabin's sheepherder's stove. After several attempts—and it does take a knack—I managed the right combination of ingredients and wood heat. Consistent results will be much easier to achieve in the "modern" kitchen.

To 1 ½ cups warm water, add 1 tablespoon of yeast (or a packet), 2 teaspoons salt, and 2 teaspoons sugar. Stir until dissolved. Allow to proof 5 minutes. Add two cups of unbleached flour and stir until well mixed—about 50 strokes. Cover and let rise until doubled. Spray a French bread pan with non-stick spray and dust with cornmeal.

Onto a floured surface, scrape out the dough, sprinkle with a little flour, and then cut in half with a dough scraper. Mix more flour into the half by working it in with the scraper. Dough will be soft. With your hands, form dough into a long rectangle, and fold once lengthwise and again. Twist and place in the pan and repeat with the other half. Slash the tops diagonally with a sharp knife and spray with water. Let the loaves rise until

doubled, then put in a pre-heated 440°
oven for about 20 minutes, until brown.

For steam, ice cubes may be placed
in bottom of your oven when you start.
The tops of the loaves may be sprayed
with water during the last five minutes of
baking for a crispier crust. Allow to cool
out of pan. Sublime are dark chocolate,
Nutella, butter, cheese, ham or jam on
this bread.

BIFTEK MIRAMONDE

*We loved this dish. The fancy name lends elegance
of place in my culinary memory bank. There is no
mistaking it. However, if you are dairy-intolerant or
cannot abide onions, as my husband, best skip it.* Tant
pis! —*as the French say, meaning, too bad. The "s" is
silent.*

1 bag of small noodles
For meat sauce: 1 ½ pounds ground
beef; thyme, bay leaf, oregano, garlic, salt
and pepper (use your instincts for
amounts.)
1 small jar cut mushrooms
Can of tomato paste
2 medium onions, chopped
1 bell pepper, chopped
1 cup celery, chopped
1 medium carton of sour cream
1 medium carton of cottage cheese
1 package of cream cheese

Cook the meat sauce as you would for spaghetti (essentially what it is). Cook the noodles and drain. In a bowl, mix the cheeses together (allow the cream cheese to come to room temperature). Place the noodles in the bottom of a round casserole dish and make a nest in the middle. Add the cheese mixture. Place the meat sauce over the top, spreading it to cover, sprinkle with parmesan cheese and bake in a 325° for 25 minutes. Mom served it with salad and French bread. I sense a pattern here.

YELLOW SQUASH CASSEROLE

As a side, this is a gorgeous dish. I have tried leaving out the onions, substituting a few garlic cloves, but it's not the same. Great for bumper crops of crooknecks. I don't put up squash, and we have ceased planting so much.

Cook 3 pounds of squash with 3 sliced onions in water, salt and pepper to taste. Drain and add 1 stick of butter and allow it to melt. In a bowl mix: 1 can of cream of chicken soup, 1 small carton of sour cream, 2 grated medium carrots, 1 small or medium jar of pimentos, depending on preference. Mix in the squash.

In a long casserole, place ½ half of a bag of bread stuffing, spread the squash mixture over it, and follow by the rest of the stuffing. Bake at 325° for 20 minutes.

SPINACH CASSEROLE

Another all-time favorite! It may also be devoured as a dip. We came to expect it for Thanksgiving and Christmas feasts, but it makes a good company side and pot luck offering.

Cook 2 packages of frozen spinach and drain as well as possible. Add: 1 stick of softened butter and 1 package of softened cream cheese (left out at room temperature). Add ½ teaspoon of lemon pepper and ½ teaspoon salt.

Chop up the contents of 2 drained jars of marinated artichokes and spread in bottom of buttered 2-quart casserole. Layer on the spinach and top this with Italian bread crumbs (seasoned). Bake at 325° for 20 minutes.

MEAT LOAF

A hearty version of the old standby, I make it to this day, occasionally substituting ground turkey.

2 eggs
¾ cup milk
2/3 cup dried bread crumbs
2 tablespoons chopped onions

¾ teaspoon salt and pepper (or to taste)

½ tablespoon dried crushed sage

1 ½ pounds ground beef

¼ cup catsup

2 tablespoons brown sugar

1 tablespoon lemon juice

1 tablespoon dry mustard

Mix ingredients (use your clean hand—it's easier). Shape into loaf or place in loaf pan. I run a line of catsup down the middle. Bake at 350° for 1 hour.

TUNA NOODLE CASSEROLE

Daughter AdriAnne requested one of her favorites when asked, and this is one I often made when she and John were growing up. Pure comfort food. May you be comforted.

3 cups noodles

¼ cup dry bread crumbs

1 tablespoon butter

1 cup chopped celery

¼ cup chopped onion

3 tablespoons butter

¼ cup flour

½ teaspoon dry mustard

1 cup milk

1 cup chicken broth

1 9 ¼ ounce can of tuna

¼ cup pimento

Cook the noodles and drain. Combine bread crumbs and 1 tablespoons of butter for later. In a skillet, cook the celery and onion in 3 tablespoons of butter until tender. Stir in the flour and mustard. Add the milk and broth all at once and cook until thickened. Mix the sauce, tuna, pimento and cooked noodles. Transfer to a 1 1/2-quart casserole. Sprinkle with crumb mixture. Bake, uncovered, at 375° for 20 minutes. Serves four.

POTATO CASSEROLE

When asked which recipe to be sure to include, our son John instantly replied, "The potato casserole!" Caveat: this is a rich dish and caution should be exercised when serving oneself.

2-pound bag frozen hash browns
½ cup butter or margarine
16-ounce carton of sour cream
1 teaspoon salt
1 teaspoon pepper
1 can cream of chicken soup
2 cups grated cheddar cheese
½ cup finely chopped onions
¼ cup additional butter
2 cups crushed cornflakes

Thaw the hash browns, then mix all the ingredients together and place in a long, buttered casserole. Melt ¼ cup butter and add 2 cups crushed cornflakes. Sprinkle this on top. Bake at 350° for 45 minutes.

STUFFED ACORN SQUASH

We grow Buttercup squash and they work just as well. This is a meal in itself.

2 Acorn or Butternut squash
1 pound of sausage, lightly browned and drained
1 teaspoon salt
¼ teaspoon pepper
1 tablespoon minced onion
½ teaspoon poultry seasoning
1 cup bread crumbs
1 egg, well-beaten
½ cup tomato sauce.

First, bake the squash at 350° until it can be easily pierced with a fork. (I split them, remove the seeds, and set them directly on the rack.) Mix the remaining ingredients and mound into hollow of each squash. Return to oven for 30 minutes, and baste with a few drops of Worcestershire sauce.

OWEN WISTER HAINE'S MINT JULEPS

While on a film shoot, my father jotted down a version of this recipe to Mr. Haine's dictation. I include it here in homage to both southern roots and Wyoming wings. You may feel as though you can fly after this libation!

Super-cold crushed ice (out of a deep freeze)

Kentucky Bourbon

White Crème de Menthe

Meyer's Rum

A heavy 1 to 1 syrup with a handful of fresh mint (1 cup sugar to 1 cup water)

Mint leaves for garnish

Muddle the mint in 1 ounce of Crème de Menthe. Strain out the mint leaves and pour remainder in a tumbler (or silver Julep Cup, if you have one). Add crushed ice, pack this down, then add 4 ounces (!*) of bourbon. Top off with more crushed ice (as a dome), and spoon 1 tablespoon of Meyer's Rum over the top. Garnish with a mint leaf and serve. *Mind, this serving is intended to last for an *entire* Kentucky Derby!

COL. PAUL LATIOLAIS' *NOTORIOUS* BBQ SAUCE

Only partly tongue-in-cheek, the making of this sauce required stamina. I see Mom pulling out her largest copper pot from France, the five-gallon behemoth, and drafting everyone to grind onions. The old meat grinder was mounted on the end of the trestle table. Mind, this was before the days of Cuisinart;

besides, the texture was all-important and the new-fangled gadget would have probably proved inadequate.

The smells in the kitchen knocked you down, open windows notwithstanding. Between the onions, garlic, and mustard, and Mom's ubiquitous Pall Malls and ever ready pot of Maxwell House coffee, it was a sense extravaganza. This recipe makes, "a lot." As this was prepared for our annual neighborhood BBQ gathering on Seminole Drive, sides appeared like loaves and fishes. Dad manned the grill after making up pitchers of Salty Dogs (gin, grapefruit juice, and salt) for the guests. Here is The Sauce—

3 pounds onions

3 heads of garlic, minced

3 bell peppers

1 bunch of celery

1 quart vegetable oil

1 jar of mustard

1 bottle of catsup

1 bottle of hot sauce (McIlhenny's Tabasco)

1 small bottle of Worcestershire sauce

Powdered red pepper *(Did I mention the recipe is spicy?)*

1 bottle of wine vinegar

Pour the oil into the pot. When heated, add the ground-up onions, celery, and peppers. Simmer for 20 minutes, then add the minced garlic and powdered red pepper. Dump in the rest (how Mom describes it), and cook it for 1

½ hours. Important: *do not* stir during the last 15 minutes. The oil will rise to the top. Ladle this off. It will be used to baste the half-chickens on the grill (skin-side down at first). Keep the sauce warm to serve on the chicken. You will need *heavy* paper plates if you're using them.

GRANDPA JOHN'S *SECRET* BBQ SAUCE

No dueling contest here, but for those whose taste buds and digestion cannot abide "heat," here is a tasty and much simpler alternative. Long regarded a "secret recipe," with all accompanying pomp, Jeff's father finally revealed the source; he'd found the instructions on a bottle of Worcestershire sauce. Jeff and I have an ongoing dispute about that pronunciation. An English couple we met in France resolved our disagreement by diplomatically calling it "Lea and Perrins." Grandpa John may have adjusted the ingredients to suit.

In a small bowl mix:
1 cup catsup
1 ½ ounces Lea and Perrins
1 ½ ounces lime juice
3 heaping tablespoons brown sugar.
Baste the meat as you grill or broil it. May be used as a marinade. Great on chicken, ribs, or just about anything.

Mom seldom baked, *but when she did* (like The World's Most Interesting Man), she relied on several tried-and-true recipes, some of which follow. Her mother, our MoMo, did bake however. At Christmastime we would receive her carefully packed box containing Christmas gifts (our yearly handmade pj's) and the world's most amazing, *interesting* cakes: a Japanese Fruit Cake *and* a Lane Cake. At MoMo's there was always either a Pound Cake nestled away in the bread box (Charleston humidity being what it was), or what she called a *plain yellow cake,* no capitals, with cocoa icing. Both mouthwatering with vanilla ice cream. I include the recipes for the latter two, and a pair of Mom's desserts.

POUND CAKE

I transcribe this recipe from a now-yellowed sheet of note paper, my grandmother's cursive hand instantly familiar. Touchstones, as loved ones are.

3 cups Swans Down cake flour
3 cups sugar
3 sticks butter
5 eggs
1 cup canned milk [evaporated]
½ teaspoon salt
½ teaspoon baking powder
2 teaspoons rum or vanilla flavoring

Cream butter, break eggs in bowl, adding one egg at a time, till all are in the batter. Alternate flour and milk as you mix. Bake at 350° for 80 minutes. [The time will depend on your altitude, I suspect. She lived at sea level. I slide a knife blade in to confirm.]

PLAIN YELLOW CAKE AND COCOA ICING

¾ cup butter
1 ½ cups sugar
2 eggs
1 ½ teaspoons vanilla
2 ½ cups flour
2 ½ teaspoons baking powder
1 teaspoon salt
1 ¼ cups milk

Cream butter, then slowly add the sugar and beat in until light and fluffy. Add the eggs, one at a time, beating well after each addition. Add the vanilla.

Sift the dry ingredients together, then add this alternately with the milk, beginning and ending with the dry ingredients. Pour into waxed paper-lined, greased and floured cake pans and bake at 350° for 30 minutes. Cool in pan for 10 minutes, then turn out onto a wire rack to complete cooling before icing.

Figure 28 Micheline Pommeret Labrousse, Photo by Nancy Latiolais Steele

COCOA ICING

4 tablespoons cocoa
1 cup brown sugar
½ stick margarine [or butter]
6 tablespoons water
½ teaspoon vanilla

Mix ingredients (except vanilla) and cook on low heat until thick. If it thickens too much, add a few drops of water after adding the vanilla to help thin to a good consistency to spread.

An obstetrics night nurse for fifteen years, Mom became fast friends with Dr. Ruth (not that Dr. Ruth) who shared baked goods with her staff on the shift. They also swapped romance novels by the shopping bag. The following is one of Dr. Ruth's recipes. Mom baked it for our daughter AdriAnne's birth on one snowy, December day in Douglas, Wyoming. It's good. It's very good. And, easy! Slice this cake thinly and wrap well to keep moist.

CHOCOLATE BUNDT CAKE

A good yellow cake mix
Chocolate instant pudding mix (small box)
4 eggs
1 cup oil
8 ounces sour cream
1 teaspoon vanilla
6 ounces chocolate chips
1 cup nuts (your choice)
Mix ingredients and bake in a tube pan at 350° for 45 minutes. Sprinkle with powdered sugar when cool.

FRESH APPLE WALNUT CAKE AND CARAMEL SAUCE

The cake is from Mom's recipe collection, and the caramel sauce came from Sr. Rita, a Benedictine nun who provided the instructions at a retreat many years ago. I pair them here for obvious reasons.

1 cup margarine [I use butter]
2 cups sugar
3 eggs
3 cups sifted all-purpose flour
1 ¼ teaspoons baking soda
¼ teaspoon salt
1 teaspoon cinnamon
2 teaspoons mace
3 cups chopped apples
2 cups chopped walnuts
½ teaspoon vanilla extract

Cream butter and sugar until fluffy. Add eggs, one at a time, beating well after each addition. Mix and sift dry ingredients. Gradually add to other. Stir in vanilla, apples, and walnuts by hand. Batter will be stiff. Spoon into greased and floured 10-inch Bundt or tube pan. Bake at 325° for 1 ½ hours. Let cool in pan for 10 minutes, then remove to rack.

SISTER RITA'S CARAMEL SAUCE

½ cup brown sugar
2 tablespoons flour
Pinch of salt
1 tablespoon butter
¼ teaspoon vanilla
1 cup water or apple juice

Combine sugar, flour, and salt in saucepan. Over medium heat, gradually stir in juice (or water). Cook and stir to a boil. Simmer and stir until thickened, remove from heat and stir in butter and vanilla.

I conclude with Mom's apple cake, mainly because I like to serve it at our apple pressing gatherings. No surprise. The caramel sauce makes for delicious caramel apples, or a dip for slices.

You may wonder at the lack of fancier fare, given the *Cordon Bleu* reference, and I do have my mother's recipe for *Coquilles St. Jacques* (for which I have her wonderful collection of scallop shells); also, *Chicken Cordon Bleu*. These instructions may be found in any number of good cookbooks, so I have omitted them in favor of more down-home fare.

While in France my parents hosted lavish dinner parties and later, stateside, but ordinary meals are what are passed down, I believe (notwithstanding Dad's *Notorious* BBQ Sauce.) In reviewing and choosing these samples, I had not anticipated the strong impressions they would make on me in sense memories—how they looked and tasted when recalled by their sources, my loved ones. I hear the squealing of the grinder as it pressed the onions—a kind of *gush-and-suck,* as we fed the machine. I see MoMo proudly slicing her cake for us after a homemade meal prepared with love, *in* love, and her stepping over to the freezer for the ever-present carton of vanilla ice cream, sometimes Neapolitan (with most of the chocolate flavor scooped out).

The fragrances and particular smells of her home return in full force—including that of the paper mill factory located nearby. And just this week, coincidentally *but* gratifyingly (*and I don't believe in coincidence*), my niece Stephanie requested any soup recipes I might have of "Mimi's."

I forwarded the French Vegetable Soup instructions and then arranged to have a food mill sent to her. To reward nostalgia? I don't think so. Rather, to encourage her. Though I didn't recognize this at the time. We can all use a healthy serving of nurturing encouragement, and nourishment. A spiral marked with cardinal points, seven generations now, I count forward to our grandchildren and back, to my mother's Alabama Grandpa and Granny.

REMEDIES

Over the years I have discovered several formulas and remedies to be useful and efficacious. An advantage to growing older—and there are many—is having had the time to experiment, make mistakes and, it is be hoped, to learn from our errors. Case in point: when a pet—normally a dog—got "skunked," I used to dash for the big can of tomato juice on hand for the purpose, but even after the dousing the horrible smell lingered. A better solution presented itself, containing hydrogen peroxide, baking soda, and a few drops of dishwashing detergent. This formula and others follow.

Nearly every year, depending on rainfall, the Saskatoon berry bushes contract a fungus as the berries set on. Easy to spot, the light purple fruits appear one day with a growth of root-like hairs on the calyx ends, the end opposite the stem. I spray the bushes liberally with a solution, hope for a sunny rest of the day, and this takes care of future infections. I have learned to employ the solution proactively, just as the fruits set on.

An environmental-friendly drain cleaner comes via Rodale Press. I've used it for decades.

Handily taped to the inside of kitchen cabinets, I post instructions for household and garden remedies, along with oft-used recipes, canning times, and herbal notes. As this manual-memoir is not meant to be classified as an herbal (a book referring to medicinal herbs and their uses), I would direct you to peruse any number of excellent sources. Since the Seventies, interest in herbal medicine has sprung up like dandelions after a spring rain. Four of my favorite practitioners/authors on the subject are Susun Weed, Rosemary Gladstar, 7 Song, and Christopher Hobbs. I have taken personal instruction from Susun, Christopher and 7 Song, but a retreat at Rosemary's Sage Mountain Farm in Vermont would be lovely someday, as would attending the Women's Southeast Herbal Conference in the North Carolina mountains.

As with any discipline, skill sets must be refreshed from time to time. The American Herbal Guild and LearningHerbs.com store a wealth of knowledge on their websites. Meanwhile, I rely mostly on medicinal herbs that grow in my immediate vicinity and their empirical study. It's only common sense. Note the difference between "culinary" and "medicinal," with regard to growing your own. However, I'm not averse to ordering non-native plants if I need to.

Happily, yarrow grows profusely here. *Wound-wort,* a nickname, is an ancient remedy, and you can learn much by its binomial, *Achillea millefolium.* Achilles, you remember, was the consummate warrior, and no doubt had cause to make use of the plant. *Millefolium* refers to the herb's countless leaves. It has antiseptic properties and two constituents that clot blood. These are only two of its many gifts. I use the tincture as a mouthwash. As an astringent, it tightens gums. Rinse well afterward.

I consider the following remedies "allies." A caveat: please learn how an herb may be contraindicated with any medication you take: e.g., *Echinacea augustifolia,* plentiful in the surrounding area, may prove problematic for those with hypothyroid issues, especially Hashimoto's Disease. For this reason, I take the tincture only when treating early symptoms of the flu (which, thankfully, neither Jeff nor I have contracted lately). Ten days on and ten days off is the usual protocol for those who wish to strengthen their immune system before symptoms present. Directions for making tinctures follow.

We've planted Elderberry bushes, of the lovely umbellifer family, whose fragrant flower sprays make a pleasant syrup in spring to add to sparkling water or prosecco. In tincture form the flowers may reduce fever. (Notice I say "may." Disclaimers require the word.) In the fall, her (flowering plants are female) purple berries are favorites of birds, so pay attention if you aim to gather some. *Do not eat the raw berries;* remember, they are toxic if uncooked. I tincture the berries (the alcohol "cooks" them by breaking open the cell walls) for use against cough and cold symptoms, and they make a delicious medicinal syrup.

Some studies suggest this remedy may not live up to its claims. However, I believe comfort and healing tap into our individual aptitudes and unique collection of cells, including a person's remarkable capacity for belief. The "placebo effect" often accounts for more than fifty percent of wellbeing in any given situation, especially with regard to perception of pain or discomfort. (See 2014 study by Kaptchuk, *Science Translational Medicine).* A teacher once suggested I place jelly beans in a jar, label it "Pain Pills," and Bob's your uncle. Placebo derives from the Latin for, "*I please."* The reverse, or "nocebo effect" operates much as a negative self-fulfilling prophecy. I compare it to a curse. Our psychology and physiology are that powerful.

Whether seeking or cultivating herbs, preparing and administering remedies, I choose to take and offer comfort in my remedies. It constitutes a spiritual practice, long exercised by those who would heal themselves and others. Intention is paramount. "Do no harm, but take no shit" is a cheeky mantra I've adopted of late, thanks to Brianna Wiest.

A remedy, remember, isn't necessarily a cure, just as healing and curing are different. Honey added to chopped sage makes a wonderful, soothing tea against a sore throat. Garlic honey spread on toast or, eaten with meat, is also effective and tasty. Fall is a good time to prepare these. Susun Weed's YouTube channel is replete with demonstrations and earthy counsel. Rosemary Gladstar also has a video presence online. Watch her own *Fire Cider* instructions.

Remedies happily encompass much more than food and medicine. I experienced a healing, associated with this place, when I first laid eyes on the property beneath the curved rimrock, an embrace of ponderosas, oaks, and ash trees. "Forest bathing," indeed. I subscribe—if erratically—to Hippocrates philosophy: "Let food be thy medicine and medicine be thy food."

A basic amount of self-care, and attention and respect paid to our core values rewards the living with old age or, as I prefer the term, *elder* status. And the secret to happiness? Aging, it seems. . . .

SKUNKED! A SOLUTION

The necessary volume will depend on the size of your pet, of course. Luckily, I haven't had cause to try this on humans, but I suspect it would help.

Into a large bowl pour a quart of hydrogen peroxide, ¼ C of baking soda, and a squirt of dish detergent. Mix well. It will foam. Leave on for five minutes after working the solution into your pet's stinky coat as thoroughly as possible, then rinse well and shampoo. You may need to repeat the procedure. I use a microfiber cloth dipped in solution on our Lab's face, avoiding his eyes.

As promised, Walt's killer fertilizer formula. Just to get it out of the way—so sweeter smells may follow. It is a remedy, after all.

WALT'S FERTILIZER

3 parts bone meal

3 parts wood ash

1 part blood meal (which can deter moles)

1 part gypsum powder. All are available in home-improvement stores or nurseries. As fertilizer and soil amendment, the mixture also loosens clay subsoil, prevalent in the area. Remember, keep it dry, or you'll be sorry!

POWDERY MILDEW SOLUTION

Many thanks to long-time friend John Curless for this simple one. We love our Saskatoon berries!

Add 1 tablespoon of baking soda and ½ teaspoon canola oil to ½ gallon of water. Put this in a small sprayer and douse the leaves and fruit once a week until the problem is gone. No more hairy berries!

GARLIC OIL SPRAY

Add three or four chopped cloves of garlic to two teaspoons of mineral oil. Allow the mix to sit for 24 hours, then strain and add the liquid to one pint of water. Add a teaspoon of dishwashing soap, and it may be diluted. Be sure to spray the underside of the leaves, where most bugs are found.

DRAIN CLEANER

1 cup baking soda
¼ cup cream of tartar
1 cup salt

Mix well. Sprinkle ¼ cup of formula over drain, followed by 1 cup boiling water. Let sit for 15 minutes. Follow with another cup of boiling water. Repeat if necessary. Keep formula in airtight container in cool place.

SILVER POLISH

Line a pan with foil, shiny side up. Add 1 tablespoon baking soda and 1 qt boiling water. Stir. Place silverware or jewelry in solution for 5-7 minutes, then into soapy water before rinsing and drying.

I smile at bright yellow, star-like flowers of St. John's Wort. They bring joy to my heart, especially because I'm not entirely sure how they wound up growing beside my Witch's Garden, home to several medicinal herbs. It's a mystery! To repeat, traditional species found in a healer's garden include rue, sage, and mints. I have added sheep sorrel, chives, valerian, and Motherwort. Hollyhock flowers lend color and edible petals. I take St. John's Wort (the word simply means "plant") against mild depression, as an anti-viral and against muscle ache.

ST. JOHN'S WORT TINCTURE
AND OIL

For a tincture, carry your jar to the flowering plant. *Hypericum perforatum* is named for the apostle (whose feast day is June 24). At this latitude some of the flowers may still be in bud stage, which is fine. A combination of buds and open flowers is best. After greeting her and asking permission, snip the top third of the flowering plant, including leaves, and carefully press the *materia* into your jar. Susun Weed suggests only pressing enough into a jar so as to make a "fairy bed." Do not cram, in other words. After, add 100 proof vodka to the top, screw on the lid, label the contents and date, then allow to infuse for six weeks, with a shake every day for ten days. You may need to top off the contents with more alcohol—the fairies having drunk some. I use small dropper bottles to administer doses. Please consult an herbal regarding dosage and frequency. The ruby red color is a natural magic when making these medicines.

SAINT JOHN'S WORT OIL

For this and other oils, the method is similar. I like to use this oil against muscle pain and sunburn.

Gather the herb (as above) into a jar, then add olive oil and use a chop stick to clear any air pockets. Oils can become rancid. Screw on a lid, label the jar, and place it in a sunny windowsill for six weeks. Take care, as some may seep out.
Strain the oil and use a cloth to squeeze the plant material of every last drop. Compost the mark (the plant material).

SAGE AND GARLIC HONEYS

I make these honeys separately, but the principle is the same.

Chop enough sage to fill a jar, its size depending upon how much you want to make, add enough honey to cover, and prick with chop stick—again, to remove air bubbles. Cap and label the contents. Allow to infuse for 12 hours at room temperature before tasting. When signs of a cold appear, use a teaspoon or more to boiling water for a soothing tea.

For garlic honey, peel (or not, your preference) enough cloves and mince to fill half a jar, then fill with honey. Stir with chop stick, cap and label, then let rest on counter for twelve hours before sampling. I'll stir the contents now and then, and keep the jar in the fridge, but it spreads better if brought out for a period.

ECHINACEA ROOT TINCTURE

Jeff and I dig Echinacea root after the fall rains, normally in November before the ground freezes. We obtained permission from a neighbor on whose property we discovered great numbers of the rosy-petaled flowers one summer. You should also ask permission from one of the larger plants. If granted, do go for the two- or three-stalked specimens, as the medicine will be more potent.

Using a long spade for the purpose, carefully dig down to pop the root loose. It's tricky to come away with an entire root, but this is all right, as it leaves the plant alive, just as we continue to live on some level, in our hearts at least, where we once lived. Memory as root. Bury the flower cone heads to reseed. Tamp the soil. We take a bucket for the roots.

Back home, clean the roots in water to remove soil, dry then cut them in ¼ inch segments. Pruners work best here. And because this is fresh material, it won't absorb and expand too much in your jar, so fill about full, ¾ at least, then add the vodka. Cap and label, then shake the mixture every day. I simply leave the root in the jar, as it only gets stronger with age. Decant some into amber dropper bottles for use.

COMFREY INFUSION

Symphytum uplandicum *is the species I planted in the large garden, a hardy perennial with big, fuzzy leaves and little purple flowers. Of the borage family, once comfrey takes hold, it's difficult to control. The leaves may be used as a compress. A common name for the plant is* knit bone, *for strengthening ligaments and bones (especially after suffering a break). Drinking an infusion on a regular basis may also help with short-term memory. Always a good thing. I add peppermint leaves to this infusion, to add flavor.*

Hang the stalks, with leaves, to dry until crisp. The shed below the house serves well for this purpose. Then, using gloves (the leaves and stalks are prickly), crush the leaves and store them away from bright light. To make the infusion, weigh out one ounce of the herb, place it into a quart jar and fill the jar with boiling water. Let steep for four to eight hours. Strain by squeezing the material, and return the liquid to jar. Cap and refrigerate. Drink the contents over two days, as it may become "off" if stored any longer.

Again, do consult an herbal for myriad more remedies and suggestions. I provide only an inkling of possibilities. We allow dandelions to proliferate in the yard, as spring greens and nectar for the bees. The sunny flowers are a cheerful tonic after winter, in the visual sense, but pretty in salads as well. I also tincture Motherwort (*Leonurus cardiaca*), a heart and uterine tonic and nourisher. She balances hormones and blood pressure, is anti-spasmodic and a nervine (calming nervous energy) and serves as a menopause ally. We delight in the yellow swathes of *shining* arnica (*Arnica fulgens*) in adjacent fields. The species is a cousin to the stronger *Arnica montana* that grows in higher elevations—on Casper Mountain, as it happens. The native species that thrives here makes an equally effective topical healing oil, or salve, if you wish to add the beeswax.

A partial list of edible plants and so-called "weeds" available in this area for foragers includes: plantain and dandelion leaves (when young), wild celery, lambs-quarter, violet leaves and flowers; Monarda bee balm, used against minor aches and pains; catnip for brewing calming teas; and chickweed, yellow-dock, and burdock root serve to cleanse the blood and assist with constipation. Do learn the difference between the death camas and wild onion; they look alike, but the onion's leaves are hollow, and (*no surprise*) it smells like an onion.

A Zen teacher shows his students a large sheet of white paper with a tiny, dark V-shape checked off to the side. "What is this?" he demands. "A bird?" someone cautiously replies. "No. It is the sky—the bird is flying through it." The lesson means to inform us about awareness.

From the opening epigraph, as falcon, storm, or perhaps a great song, the poet Rilke's "I" continues to spiral in the vast expanse. By now, you may have recognized that those attributes, distinguishing a swiftly diving bird, tempestuous weather, or music of the spheres, might each conspire to hold us accountable to life. How can one *not* respond? Whether you live in a remote countryside, the suburbs, or in a town, similarly difficult forces—and choices—come to bear. Their elements are only slightly tweaked.

May this homestead manual and memoir be received as a kind of *Brig O'Doon* crossing, between sensibilities, to bridge them, not in place of stark reality, but more a considered version of such: my olive branch to life, if you will, proffered in the name of peace. . . .

With deep bows, best wishes, and every green blessing to you for health and happiness, this crofter takes her leave, fragrant cup of linden tea in hand, to go sit outdoors, inhale and turn her face to a pale winter sky. A single exhalation from a black crow pierces milky silence.

CHECKLISTS

SPRINGTIME

- Prune the fruit trees and shrubs.
- Spray the apple trees against fire blight.
- Prune the grape vines.
- Grind the small diameter limbs and twigs, and mulch the trees and shrubs.
- Till the garden after amending the soil. *We mainly use peat moss.*
- Begin the weeding.
- Replant or plant new trees, shrubs, and perennials.
- Set out the rain gauge.
- Plant garden(s) near June 1. *(In our area, recall that certain varieties require a certain number of days to mature. This information is generally found on seed packets, but also remember, it is soil temperature that determines germination and the number of days to maturity.)*
- Consider road maintenance needs.
- Re-stain wooden structures, if necessary.
- Make inventory of frozen or canned goods.
- Replace the furnace filter.
- Make appointment with water conditioning company for service man to replace the filters on reverse osmosis unit, and to check the water softener.

o Perform hot tub maintenance (if applicable).

o Schedule personal health physicals, eye exams, and dentist appointments.

o Check the perimeter of the enclosed gardens and orchard for anything amiss, including downed electric fence.

o Continue to set traps for mice and packrats.

o As temperatures rise, watch for rattlesnakes.

o Remember to just sit on occasion and admire the blooming orchard!

Figure 29 The nation's first national monument is known by many names: Bear Lodge, Tree Rock, Tsao-Ai, Grey-Horned Butte, Mato Tipila, among others, by Native Americans. "Devils Tower" remains a mistranslation.

SUMMERTIME

o Unclutter. *Ceaselessly holding the intention goes a long way toward actual execution.*

o Begin watering schedule when necessary.

o Air the pillows and comforters. *Sunshine sanitizes.*

o Wash the windows and steam the carpets.

o Thin the seedlings in the vegetable and flower gardens as needed.

o Forage for edible wild herbs and plants.

o Watch for insect infestations and either cut away, pick off by hand, or spray with a non-toxic solution. *Tent caterpillars sneak onto higher limbs of chokecherries, their industrious webs housing a nursery. Cut these away and dispose.*

o Harvest pie cherries, pit, and freeze. Make a cherry pie!

o As they ripen, juice grapes and tomatoes, if desired.

o Harvest the garlic crop. Make garlic braids or not, but hang any garlic to cure for two weeks in the warm garage. *Local farmers' markets take them.*

o Hoe the root crops.

o Thin young apples to one or two per stem.

o Mow the lawn as needed. Change the mower blades and oil as required.

o Inspect home and outbuildings for damage, or need for repair.

o Fertilize the plantings regularly.

o Sharpen the hoe and spade. Oil them against rust. *This may be done anytime.*

o Prepare for houseguests, as summer invites them.

o Take a day off once in a while to visit a lake, the mountains, or other restorative location. Essential! *Running errands in town does not count.*

o Early summer allows for travel, before chores become time-sensitive.

o Take advantage of a lull in activities.

o Order propane for the buried tank, to obtain the best price of the year, and have smaller auxiliary tanks filled.

Figure 31 Heed Kitchen Witches!

AUTUMN

o Harvest the garden produce, vineyard, and orchard as vegetables and fruits ripen. Engage help if necessary. Advertise locally. *Post sign in town and beside mailbox.*

o Inspect canner rubber seal for degradation (rub Vaseline on it yearly), and test the steam valve. Can, freeze, or dehydrate the harvested produce. Make jams and jellies. *Give away extras, and remember to feast!*

o Press apples into cider.

o Take apples and grapes to local farmers' markets.

o Continue to check mouse traps and/or set out live traps for critters, such as packrats and raccoons, if evidence of their mischief appears—*such as an entire row of garlic leaves nibbled to the ground!*

o Clean stovepipes and gutters.

o Check the light bulb in the well housing.

o Plug in the heat tape on the back porch, against softener pipe freeze-ups.

o Before a hard freeze, drain the hoses and turn off the water to outside house faucets.

o Fertilize certain plants (bulbs), trees and shrubs.

o Continue to organize and unclutter!

o Cut firewood, split and stack it for winter.

o Till the garden after the crops are harvested. *Some plant a winter cover crop. We do not.*

- ○ Plant garlic cloves for the following year.
- ○ Tidy the lawn with one last mowing.
- ○ Shut garage windows, vent in studio/atrium, and bring in outdoor potted plants for winter.
- ○ Dig *Echinacea* roots to make tincture. Also, if so inclined, make herbal tinctures, salves, vinegars, and oils as specific plants mature.
- ○ Continue to be on guard against rattlesnakes.
- ○ Admire the magnificent fall colors.

WINTER

o Continue uncluttering and organizing tasks. *Notice a pattern here?*

o Confirm the tractor battery is properly plugged in and charging.

o Feed the birds. We find that sunflower seeds satisfy most species.

o If the opportunity for travel presents itself, and depending on the length of time away, consider turning off all water, to protect against freeze-ups.

o While not a homestead chore per se, winter celebrations require a thoughtful dose of preparation, and Yuletide's star shines brightest on the treetop. *Simplicity serves here.*

o Preparing taxes, penning long rambling letters, and reading for delicious stretches of time may be enjoyed with the more leisurely pace.

o Continue monitoring the mouse traps.

o Contemplate the weighty issues, now that you have time, but strive for equanimity if at all possible. Synonyms include "composure," "calmness" and "calm."

o Peruse photograph albums, school yearbooks, and saved letters. *For perspective.*

o Put the greenhouse to bed until springtime.

o Take hikes into the surrounding woods, now that snakes are dormant. *(Ticks bedevil deer, often latching on through the winter months, hence, the wee meanies drop onto the convenient deer trails that crisscross the land.)*

o In late winter, a thaw presents an opportunity to paint the apple tree trunks white against the too-early warm snap. *The paint lasts several years.*

o Cook soups, bake bread, and experiment with new recipes. *Invite friends to dinner.*

o Gently practice your arts, enjoy long phone conversations, and mainly, rest. Lie near fallow in this season, at least as far as you are able. Recharge. My own writing reflects a more introspective and concentrated aspect during the quiet months, as though I'm plugged into a trickle charger, like the tractor's.

o If your employment takes you elsewhere, upon your return each day embrace winter with care, attention, and a purposeful resolve to "winter well."

o Nurture yourself and others. *Yours is the animating spirit of your home.*

o Finally, remember to wear cleats when traversing icy sidewalks, paths, and roads.

ACKNOWLEDGMENTS

Owing much to others, here I am granted the opportunity to "put it in writing." A rewarding exercise in any circumstance. A *taking stock,* a reckoning, and a meditation on gratitude, first, to my brothers and sisters, for your love and friendship over the years. And to David, who is caring for sweet sister Felicia, you teach us the meaning of devotion.

With the times, there have arisen marked differences of opinion and worldview. May we continue to invoke and respect the bottom line, the inextricable fact—the *truth* of our connection. If one of us needs a "walkabout," then fine, let her go, then upon her return, let us welcome home the prodigal. Tongue firmly planted in cheek.

"Freedom's just another word for nothin' left to lose,

Nothin' ain't worth nothin' but it's free. . ." wrote Kris Kristofferson.

To my husband Jeff, a million thanks for your faithful imaginings of our life, as we once dreamed it. In reviewing the manuscript before publication, I suspect you wondered who this character was I'd drawn as yourself. You are that and so much more.

To our children, Adri and John and your loved ones—Joe, Sami, Parker, Austin, and Haven—I live in awe of your collective bravery, strength, and love. Thanks for everything. Adri, for reviewing the manuscript, for offering insights and suggestions, and—

for suggesting a longed-for trip to Scotland and Paris after the pandemic restrictions, *thank you*. My childhood's French "Mary Poppins," Micheline, died earlier this year after suffering two strokes. We'd spoken about six weeks earlier, her good humor rising intact above her difficult circumstances. I miss her sorely. A purpose of our trip to France—to visit her and her daughter Paola's resting place, to lay flowers, to bid farewell, and to offer thanks.

To my wonderful editor, Sarah Pridgeon, who so generously provided a moving Foreword—I am indebted. I discovered a treasure in my own backyard, a modern-day settler *all the way* from England. Fortune smiled.

To my friend and neighbor, Andi Hummel, for the read-through, I am most grateful. Your suggestions were spot-on.

To long-time friend Linda Spears, another early reader, for your exquisite eye and insights; Deep Bows, as always. May your backyard bell chime peacefully, always.

To Joan Fullerton, friend and artist of Intuitive Landscapes, among others, thank you for providing an exquisite cover image, for helping me *see* and *feel* joy.

To those working so very hard to ease the suffering of others during the pandemic; to those striving with every fiber of their being to pull our nation forward after multiple catastrophes (and continuing to threaten as of this writing), I salute you in gratitude.

Many thanks and deep bows to the Wyoming Arts Council and National Endowment for the Arts for awarding me the developmental grant, and—for all you do for our state—heartfelt kudos.

My initial purpose in writing CROFTER (as a roadmap for whoever finds themselves here one day) has evolved, it seems, to include a greater motive—to entice others to plant seeds of goodwill and compassion, as well as those of fresh produce and traditional healing medicinals.

I thank the Earth, our home. Regarding memory and memoir, the land heals broken hearts, if allowed. I invite you to consider the possibility with me.

Finally, I am grateful for this *practice* of writing. It delivers much more joy than merely viewing one's efforts in print. And last (but hardly least!), to my readers, thanks for listening, as it were. I hope you heard an answer or two, no matter the question.

Figure 32 Gabe, as a pup, asking the question.

ABOUT THE AUTHOR

Renée and her husband live rurally in northeast Wyoming where they tend an orchard, a large garden, and much garlic. Their children are grown and live out-of-state. She is a past recipient of the Frank Nelson Doubleday Memorial Award, awarded by the Wyoming Arts Council and NEA.

A folk musician, she plays the odd performance, enjoys Zen, knitting, taking walks, visiting friends, family, and national parks when possible.

Her *Riven Country* series is set mainly in Wyoming. A collection of creative non-fiction essays, *A Singular Notion*, was published in 2006 by Pronghorn Press. In 2010 she compiled, edited and published her late father's early aviation memoir, *STRAIGHT AND LEVEL, The True Story of a Young Man's Quest to Become a Flying Cadet in the U. S. Air Corps.*

CROFTER describes life on a small rural homestead, disguised as pages of a manual. Amended by recollections of her Air Force childhood, Carrier stretches memory decades into the now.

"My faculty of reason quakes with possible and less mad futures, while simultaneously wrestling small fears. *May peace prevail* remains my fervent prayer."

Made in the USA
Monee, IL
26 September 2023

43478548R00142